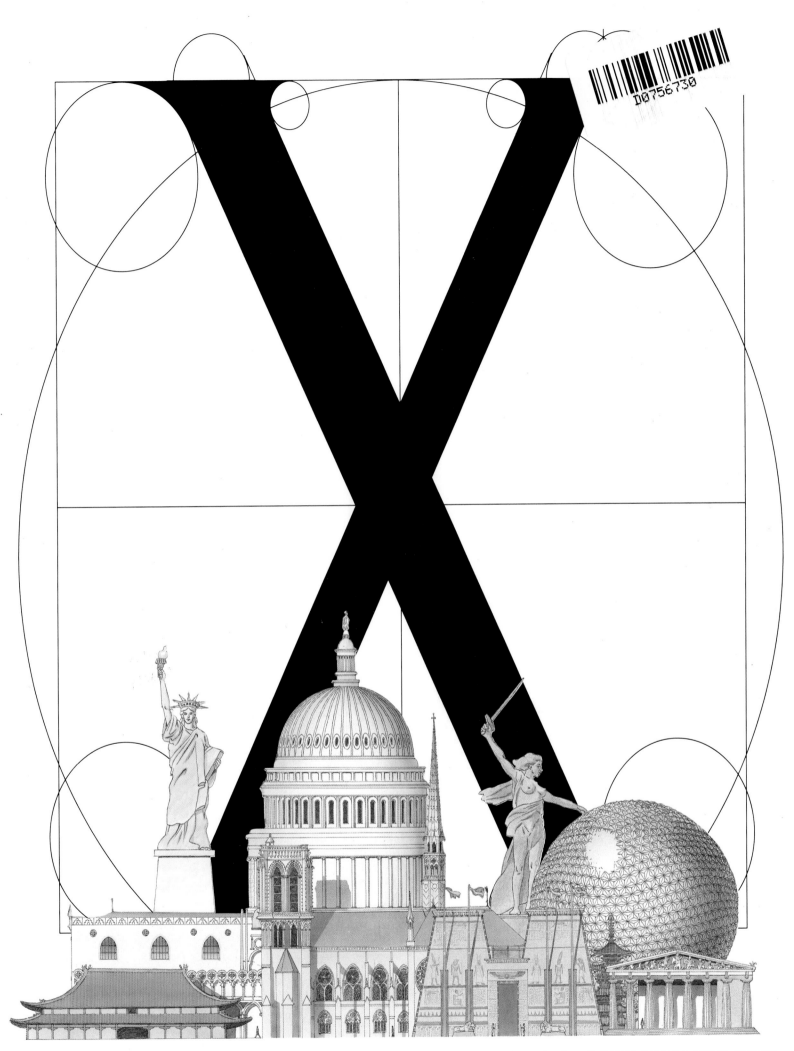

THE X-RAY PICTURE BOOK *of* BIG BUILDINGS *of the* MODERN WORLD

Creator:

David Salariya was born in Dundee, Scotland, where he studied illustration and printmaking, concentrating on book design in his post-graduate year. He has illustrated a wide range of books on botanical, historical and mythical subjects. He has designed and created the *Timelines*, *New View* and *X-Ray Picture Book* series for Watts. He lives in Brighton with his wife, the illustrator Shirley Willis.

Author:

Joanne Jessop holds an undergraduate degree from the University of Waterloo in Ontario, Canada, and a master's degree from the University of British Columbia in Canada. She has many years' experience as a writer and editor of children's information books. She has also written *The X-Ray Picture Book of Big Buildings of the Ancient World*.

First published in 1994
by Franklin Watts

Franklin Watts
95 Madison Avenue
New York, NY 10016

David Salariya — *Series Editor*
Ruth Taylor — *Senior Editor*
Diana Holubowicz — *Editor*

Artists:

Mark Bergin
Nick Hewetson
John James
Mark Peppe
Gerald Wood

Artists

Mark Bergin 10-11, 12-13, 18-19, 20-21, 22-23, 30-31; **Nick Hewetson** 6-7, 8-9, 32-33, 38-39, 40-41, 42-43, 44-45; **John James** 14-15, 16-17, 26-27; **Mark Peppe** 24-25, 34-35, 36-37; **Gerald Wood** 28-29.

Printed in Belgium

The X-RAY PICTURE BOOK of BIG BUILDINGS of the MODERN WORLD

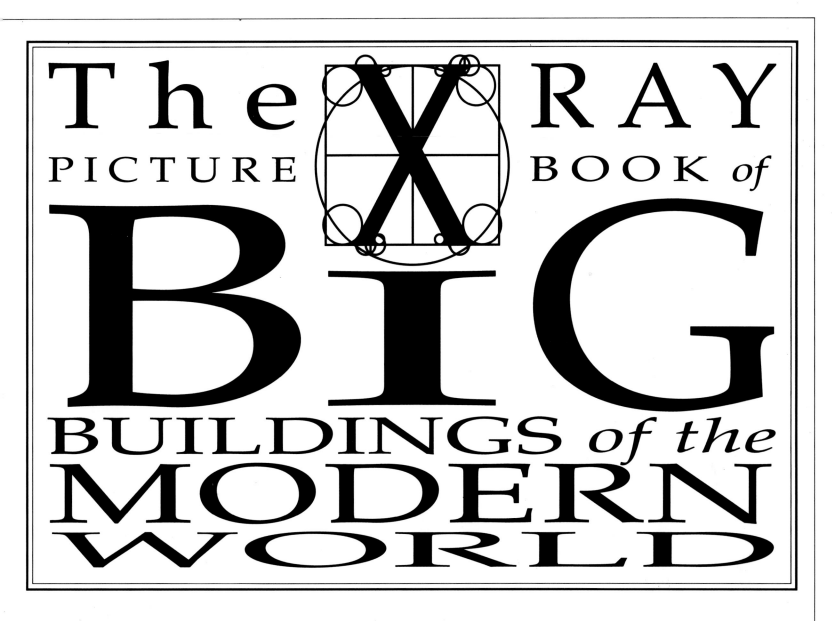

Created and designed by
DAVID SALARIYA

Written by
JOANNE JESSOP

FRANKLIN WATTS

NEW YORK · CHICAGO · LONDON · TORONTO · SYDNEY

CONTENTS

THE ROYAL PAVILION

STATUE OF LIBERTY

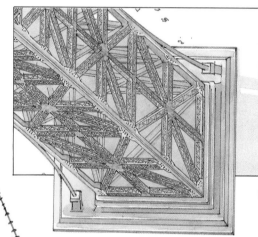

THE EIFFEL TOWER

TOWER BRIDGE

EMPIRE STATE BUILDING
& OTHER SKYSCRAPERS

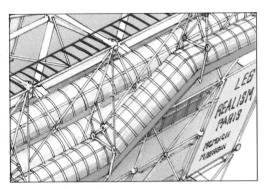
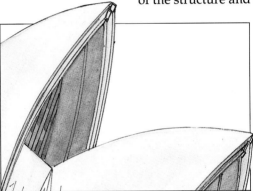
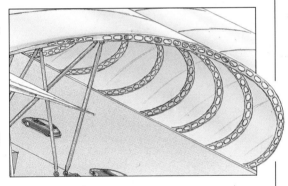

THE ROYAL PAVILION

THE STORY OF THE ROYAL PAVILION began in 1786, when George, the Prince of Wales, later to become Britain's King George IV, took up residence in a farmhouse in Brighton, England. He loved the excitement and informality of this seaside resort, which was in sharp contrast to the formality of royal life. But he soon found that the simple farmhouse did not suit his exotic taste for luxury, and within a year, he had embarked upon the first of a series of building projects that were to span the next thirty-five years. The prince's inspiration and exuberance, combined with the skills of the architect, John Nash, and the interior designers, Frederick Crace and Robert Janes, were to transform the modest farmhouse into an extraordinary Oriental fantasy, known as the Royal Pavilion.

George, the Prince of Wales, was born in 1762 and became Prince Regent in 1811. In 1820, he finally succeeded to the throne as King George IV. He died in 1830.

In 1787, the Brighton farmhouse underwent its first transformation. The existing building was extended to include a large domed circular drawing room with rooms to the north and south; these were bounded on the west by a long corridor.

Brighton in 1783, when George, the Prince of Wales, first visited, was a carefree and exciting place for those with leisure time and wealth. They came here to enjoy the health benefits of bathing in (and even drinking) sea water, as recommended by Dr. Russel of nearby Lewes. In the process, they turned the small fishing village of Brighton into the first seaside resort.

England

Brighton is on the south coast of England, about 50 miles (about 80 km) from London.

The focal point of the Banqueting Room is an enormous winged dragon that clutches the central gasolier (a gaslight chandelier) in its claws. The gasolier has a ring of 6 more dragons, each supporting a lotus-petal lamp.

Minaret

The Great Kitchen was furnished with every convenience available. There was hot and cold running water and numerous ovens for stewing, roasting and baking. The central table was heated with steam running through concealed pipes. The roasting spit rotated automatically, powered by the rising heat of the fire. Tent-like copper canopies over the ovens carried away excess vapor. The slender cast-iron support columns, fashioned into palm trees and topped with copper palm leaves, carried the Oriental theme into the Great Kitchen.

The exterior of the Pavilion, with its Indian-style domes, arches and minarets, and its Chinese-style interior known as chinoiserie, were not to everyone's taste. There were many insulting comments about the Pavilion's extraordinary appearance, and the prince's close involvement in every detail of the design and decoration was considered a frivolous preoccupation for a man in his position. But George, the Prince of Wales, was not deterred by such criticism and the Royal Pavilion was to become his own personal creation – a folly as extravagant as the prince himself.

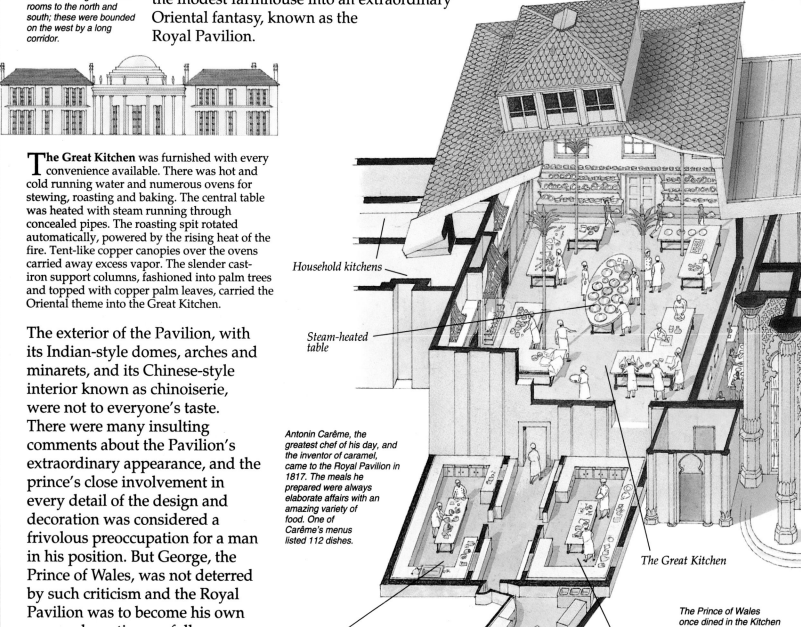

Household kitchens

Steam-heated table

Antonin Carême, the greatest chef of his day, and the inventor of caramel, came to the Royal Pavilion in 1817. The meals he prepared were always elaborate affairs with an amazing variety of food. One of Carême's menus listed 112 dishes.

The Great Kitchen

Pantry

Restroom

Pantry

The Prince of Wales once dined in the Kitchen with his servants. A red cloth was laid on the flagstone floor for the occasion.

In the Banqueting Room, the 46 foot-high (14 m) domed ceiling is decorated with lifelike paintings of gigantic plantain leaves, some formed three-dimensionally in copper. A small lotus-leaf chandelier hangs in each corner of the room attached to a mythological Chinese bird known as Fum. The murals depict scenes from Chinese life.

Mastic (a type of cement) was used in the stucco rendering with disastrous results. The mastic was not sufficiently waterproof to prevent leaking, and there was considerable damage to the interior decoration. In 1827, the tent roofs were recovered with copper.

Gasolier

Tent roof

Onion-shaped dome

Skylights

The walls were constructed of brick and covered with stucco, which was streaked with color to resemble blocks of stone. This was a very laborious process and difficult to maintain; therefore, it was soon abandoned in favor of using plain stucco.

Bedroom

Lotus leaf

Dragon

Balcony

South Drawing Room

Iron support

A formal dinner in the Banqueting Room could last up to 4 hours. Musicians in an adjoining room would provide music for the dinner guests.

The enormous gasolier was powered by the new discovery of the day – gas. Jets of gas were piped along the walls and ceiling directly into the lamps of the gasolier.

The dinner guests could relax with cards and conversation in the South Drawing Room, where the walls were decorated in gold leaf. The support columns in the room take the form of palm trees.

Onion-shaped dome

In 1803, George, the Prince of Wales, had new stables built. The architect, William Porden, chose an Indian style with a large domed roof. In 1815, when John Nash was hired to extend the Royal Pavilion, the same Indian style used in the picturesque and luxurious stables was chosen for the Pavilion itself.

The huge central dome and the two tentlike roofs at each end are surrounded by soaring towers in the style of Muslim minarets.

Chimneys

Cast-iron framework supporting the dome

Saloon

Corridor (lower floor)

The Saloon is decorated with Indian motifs. It is a high-domed, circular room extended by 2 semi-circular apses.

Indian-style arched windows

Dressing Room

North Drawing Room

Balcony

Bedroom

Stone tracery

The North Drawing Room was used for informal late suppers, and the columns in this room were topped with umbrellalike canopies with gilded serpents winding around the columns.

Skylight

Minaret

Chimneys

Serpent

Organ pipes

Music Room

THE ROYAL PAVILION

THE ROYAL PAVILION is remarkable not only in appearance, but also in construction. Nash used the most advanced technology of his day. Cast iron was first used as a building material with great success in France in 1809. Nash used it in the construction of the Royal Pavilion. There are huge iron supports within the walls of the building to carry the weight of the cast-iron framework, which supports the central dome. Sheet iron is used as the skin for the domes, and the tent roofs, which were originally covered in mastic, were eventually re-covered in copper. The decorative possibilities when using cast iron were far wider than when using any other building material available at the time, and it was used in the Royal Pavilion to give interiors a light and airy appearance. Cast iron was also used to make the decorative, yet strong, support columns and delicate imitation bamboo staircases.

George, the Prince of Wales, had a preference for an Indian-style exterior, which reflected the growing interest in Indian art and architecture at a time when England was gaining political and economic power over India. Although Nash's domes were inspired by Mogul buildings of the seventeenth and eighteenth centuries, they were unlike anything found in the East. The domes, the slender minarets, and the arched window frames are architectural fantasies unique to the Royal Pavilion.

The corridor downstairs, which is lit only by skylights, runs through the center of the Royal Pavilion. It leads to the Banqueting, Music and Drawing Rooms. The corridor is decorated in pinks, blues, reds, and amber, and is the most Chinese part of the Royal Pavilion.

The Music Room is the most elaborate example of the Pavilion's chinoiserie decor. The room is dominated by glowing red murals, canopies and doors.

King's Bedroom

In 1820, the aging Prince of Wales became King George IV. By then he was so overweight and crippled with gout that climbing the stairs had become difficult. The King's Apartments were the last addition to the Royal Pavilion. Built at ground level, the Apartments consisted of an anteroom, the King's Library, the Bedroom with its concealed private staircase, a Dressing Room, a Page's Room, and a splendid marble-and-mahogany bathroom with water that was pumped directly from the sea.

STATUE OF LIBERTY

New York City is on the East Coast of the United States.

New York

New York City is on the East Coast of the United States.

The 7 spikes of Liberty's crown represent the 7 continents and the 7 seas of the world.

The spiral staircase: 171 steps to the observation platform in the crown.

Inside the head

Windows

Observation deck

FOR OVER A HUNDRED YEARS, THE STATUE of Liberty has stood as a welcoming beacon for Americans returning home and for thousands of immigrants seeking a new life in a new land. Liberty, the most famous of American landmarks, was the creation of a group of Frenchmen, including the sculptor Bartholdi, who first discussed the idea at a dinner party in 1865. The French had helped the Americans in their struggle for independence from Britain and were now themselves establishing France as an independent republic after years of political turmoil. The statue was to commemorate the 100th anniversary of American independence and stand as a monument to the republican ideals of liberty and equality that both countries shared. Twenty-one years later, having missed the centenary of American independence, the Statue of Liberty was erected in New York Harbor, a gift from the people of France to the people of the United States.

The Statue of Liberty, from its toes to the tip of its torch, is 151 feet (46 m) tall; including the pedestal, it rises to a height of 305 feet (93 m). It weighs 204 tons, the outer covering of copper accounting for nearly half that weight. Liberty's face is 10 feet (3 m) from ear to ear; her nose is over 3 feet (1 m) long.

Liberty holds a tablet with July 4, 1776, the date the United States declared independence, written in Roman numerals.

Inscription

Tablet

Her eyes are 2.6 feet (0.8 m) wide.

The face of the Statue of Liberty is 10 feet (3 m) wide.

Electric lamps around the platform of the torch were to serve as a lighthouse. But it was thought the rays would reflect off clouds and confuse ships. The lamps were placed inside the torch's flame, which was pierced with holes, but this made the light too feeble for use in a lighthouse.

Torch

Her arm is 43 feet (13 m) long.

Copper outer covering

The Statue of Liberty is a hollow structure. Four wrought-iron posts, slightly angled towards each other and held rigid by horizontal and diagonal bracing struts, form the central pylon. A similar, but smaller, structure is attached to the upper part of the pylon to form the central core of the raised arm. Stretching out from the central supporting pylon, in the approximate shape of the statue, is a secondary framework. Hundreds of flat, thin iron bars are attached at one end to the secondary framework and at the other end to a webbing of metal straps on the inside of the copper outer covering. Because the iron bars are flexible, Liberty's copper skin can expand and contract in response to heat and cold, and it can adapt itself to changes in the wind.

Wrought-iron posts

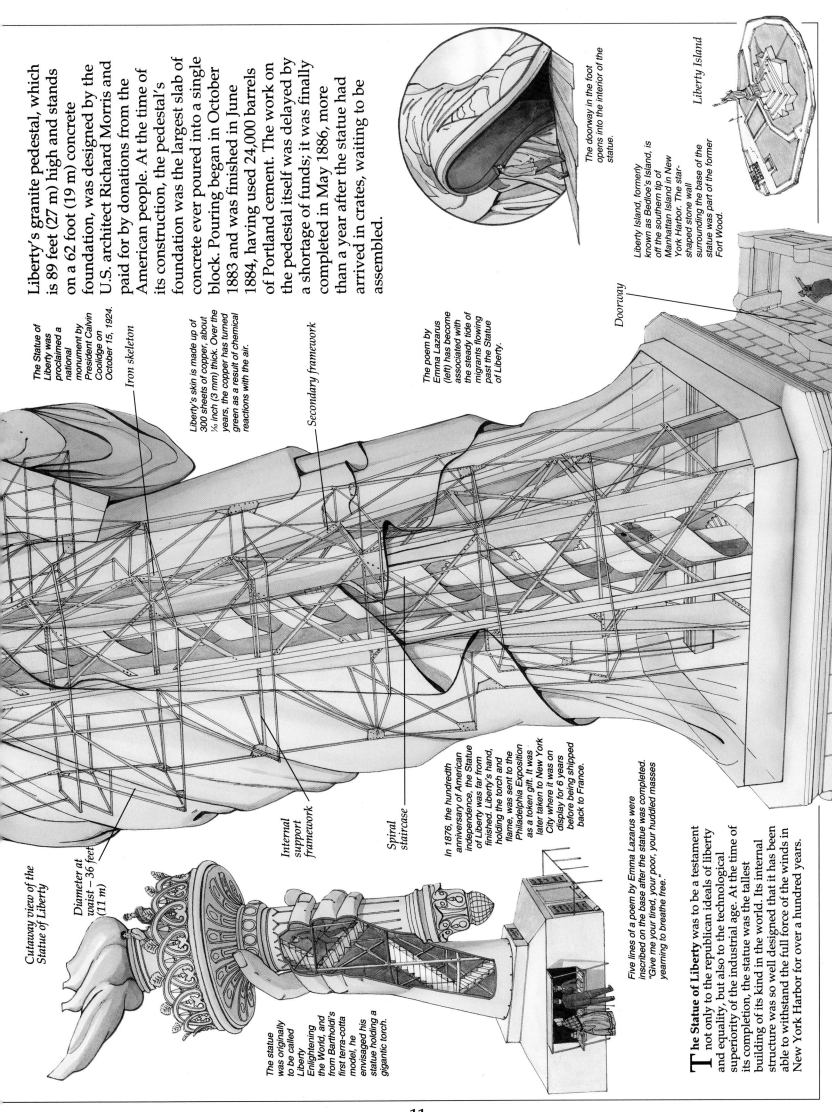

Liberty's granite pedestal, which is 89 feet (27 m) high and stands on a 62 foot (19 m) concrete foundation, was designed by the U.S. architect Richard Morris and paid for by donations from the American people. At the time of its construction, the pedestal's foundation was the largest slab of concrete ever poured into a single block. Pouring began in October 1883 and was finished in June 1884, having used 24,000 barrels of Portland cement. The work on the pedestal itself was delayed by a shortage of funds; it was finally completed in May 1886, more than a year after the statue had arrived in crates, waiting to be assembled.

The doorway in the foot opens into the interior of the statue.

Liberty Island

Liberty Island, formerly known as Bedloe's Island, is off the southern tip of Manhattan Island in New York Harbor. The star-shaped stone wall surrounding the base of the statue was part of the former Fort Wood.

Doorway

The Statue of Liberty was proclaimed a national monument by President Calvin Coolidge on October 15, 1924.

Iron skeleton

Liberty's skin is made up of 300 sheets of copper, about ⅛ inch (3 mm) thick. Over the years, the copper has turned green as a result of chemical reactions with the air.

Secondary framework

The poem by Emma Lazarus (left) has become associated with the steady tide of migrants flowing past the Statue of Liberty.

Cutaway view of the Statue of Liberty

Diameter at waist – 36 feet (11 m)

The statue was originally to be called Liberty Enlightening the World, and from Bartholdi's first terra-cotta model, he envisaged his statue holding a gigantic torch.

Internal support framework

Spiral staircase

In 1876, the hundredth anniversary of American independence, the Statue of Liberty was far from finished. Liberty's hand, holding the torch and flame, was sent to the Philadelphia Exposition as a token gift. It was later taken to New York City where it was on display for 6 years before being shipped back to France.

Five lines of a poem by Emma Lazarus were inscribed on the base after the statue was completed. "Give me your tired, your poor, your huddled masses yearning to breathe free."

The Statue of Liberty was to be a testament not only to the republican ideals of liberty and equality, but also to the technological superiority of the industrial age. At the time of its completion, the statue was the tallest building of its kind in the world. Its internal structure was so well designed that it has been able to withstand the full force of the winds in New York Harbor for over a hundred years.

Terra-cotta models

Bartholdi then made a plaster model twice the size of the terra-cotta original, checked the proportions and enlarged it twice more until it was one-fourth the size of the final statue. This was then taken apart piece by piece, and using precise measurements each section was separately enlarged to the full size. Large pieces of wood were carefully sculpted and shaped to fit around the plaster sections.

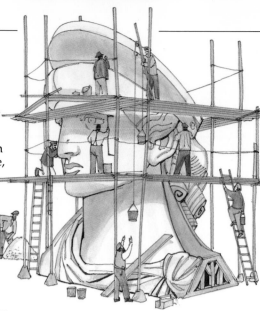

A system of ropes and buckets lifted plaster to the workmen covering the statue.

In deciding on a final design for the Statue of Liberty, Bartholdi made several terra-cotta models. He drew on ancient Roman symbolism of Liberty as a woman, and his figures held aloft the light of truth.

BUILDING THE
Statue of Liberty

THE DESIGNER OF THE STATUE OF LIBERTY was Frédéric-Auguste Bartholdi. He was a well-known sculptor of his day and, throughout the twenty-one years of the statue's construction, a tireless fund-raiser. Liberty's ingenious internal structure was the creation of Alexandre-Gustave Eiffel, a specialist in iron-and-steel structures, whose work would eventually include the Eiffel Tower, in Paris.

The internal design combines the strength of the central pylon with a flexible secondary framework which allows the statue to sway about 3 inches (almost 8 cm) in 50 mph (80 km/h) winds.

When the pieces of wood were removed they formed a perfect mold for the parts of the statue they had covered. Thin sheets of copper were then hammered into these molds. The copper was shaped first by bending it with levers and then hammering it inside the wooden mold. The finishing was done with smaller hammers and smoothing tools.

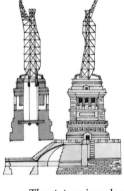

The statue rises above the Paris skyline

REPUBLIQUE FRANCAISE
30ᶠ+10ᶠ 1834 BARTHOLDI 1904 POSTES

A French postage stamp showing Bartholdi and his statue.

To ensure that the building process would work, the statue was temporarily assembled in the courtyard of Gaget and Gauthier. Only one in ten rivets in the copper skin was used so that it could be easily taken apart and packed into 210 crates for shipment to New York.

Over 9,000 separate measurements were required to enlarge the final sections of the statue. Each fingernail alone needed 6 measurements – 3 on the smaller model and 3 on the enlargement.

Building the Statue of Liberty was an enormous feat of technical engineering. The statue was enlarged step-by-step from the original terra-cotta model to its full size of almost 305 feet (93 m). For this enlargement process, thousands of precise calculations and measurements were required. Had any one of the measurements been inaccurate, the enlarged segments of the statue would not have fitted together properly and work on the statue would have been delayed by months.

When Bartholdi first began working on the full-size hand and torch of the Statue of Liberty, reporters and dozens of spectators filled the courtyard at the workshop of Gaget and Gauthier to watch the creation of this immense sculpture.

Raising the head

Iron straps, forged to follow the contours of the copper covering, were attached to the inside of the copper sheets with countersunk rivets that were invisible from the outside. Thin iron bars joined the iron straps to the internal framework.

When Bartholdi first saw Bedloe's Island he thought it would make the perfect setting for his immense statue.

Liberty Island

The faces of George Washington, Thomas Jefferson, Abraham Lincoln and Theodore Roosevelt were carved into the side of Mount Rushmore between 1927 and 1941.

Mount Rushmore

Throughout history people have built colossal statues as monuments to their gods and heroes. The statue of Lord Bahubali, in India, is the tallest statue ever to be carved out of a single piece of rock. It stands 56 feet (17 m) tall. The faces of 4 presidents are carved into the side of Mount Rushmore in South Dakota. It is the largest sculpture carved out of a rock cliff, and the presidents' faces are each 59 feet (18 m) high. Today, the world's largest full-figure statue is the 269-foot (82-m)-high concrete Motherland statue in Russia.

Motherland statue

The Motherland statue, built between 1959 and 1967, is the centerpiece of a huge war memorial that commemorates the former Soviet Republic's victory in World War II.

Giant statue of Lord Bahubali

The Statue of Lord Bahubali, created about A.D. 981, is a sacred image for the followers of the Jaina religion.

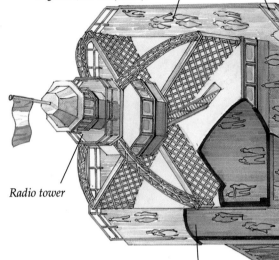

Alexandre-Gustave Eiffel had a finely furnished private studio (below) situated at the top of the Eiffel Tower

Paris is the capital of France, and is situated in the northeast of the country. The Eiffel Tower is on the left bank of the River Seine, which runs through Paris.

France

In 1959, a radio antenna was placed on the top of the Tower, raising its height to 1,050 feet (320 m).

Third platform

Observation deck

Radio tower

Restaurant

THE EIFFEL TOWER

THE EIFFEL TOWER WAS BUILT to serve as the entrance archway to the Paris Exhibition of 1889, held in celebration of the hundredth anniversary of the French Revolution. The Tower was as innovative as it was controversial.

Iron and steel tended to be used mainly for industrial purposes, such as building bridges, and railway stations, but some designers chose to use the materials in a more experimental way. Alexandre-Gustave Eiffel wanted to use the engineering skills of the industrial age to erect the world's tallest building. At that time, the biggest structure was the Washington Monument in Washington D.C., a 554-foot (169-m)-high stone obelisk erected in 1884. Eiffel's tower of 1,000 feet (300 m) was to be almost twice as high.

The upper platform, which could accommodate up to 800 people, allowed visitors a panoramic view of Paris. Above this were several rooms for scientific research into aerodynamics, telegraphy and meteorology.

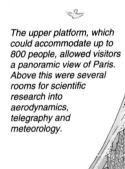

There were 4 double-decker glass-encased elevators to the first platform. Two more elevators ran to the second platform. Another elevator carried passengers to the top. All the elevators were operated by hydraulic power. The ascent took just 7 minutes; 2,350 passengers could be carried to the top every hour.

Wrought-iron latticework

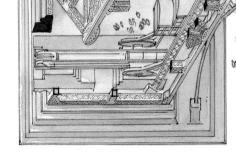

In March 1889 the Eiffel Tower was opened by a small group of dignitaries, who climbed the 1,792 steps and hoisted the French flag.

Originally, there were large restaurants, a 250-seat theater and other facilities on the first floor of the Eiffel Tower.

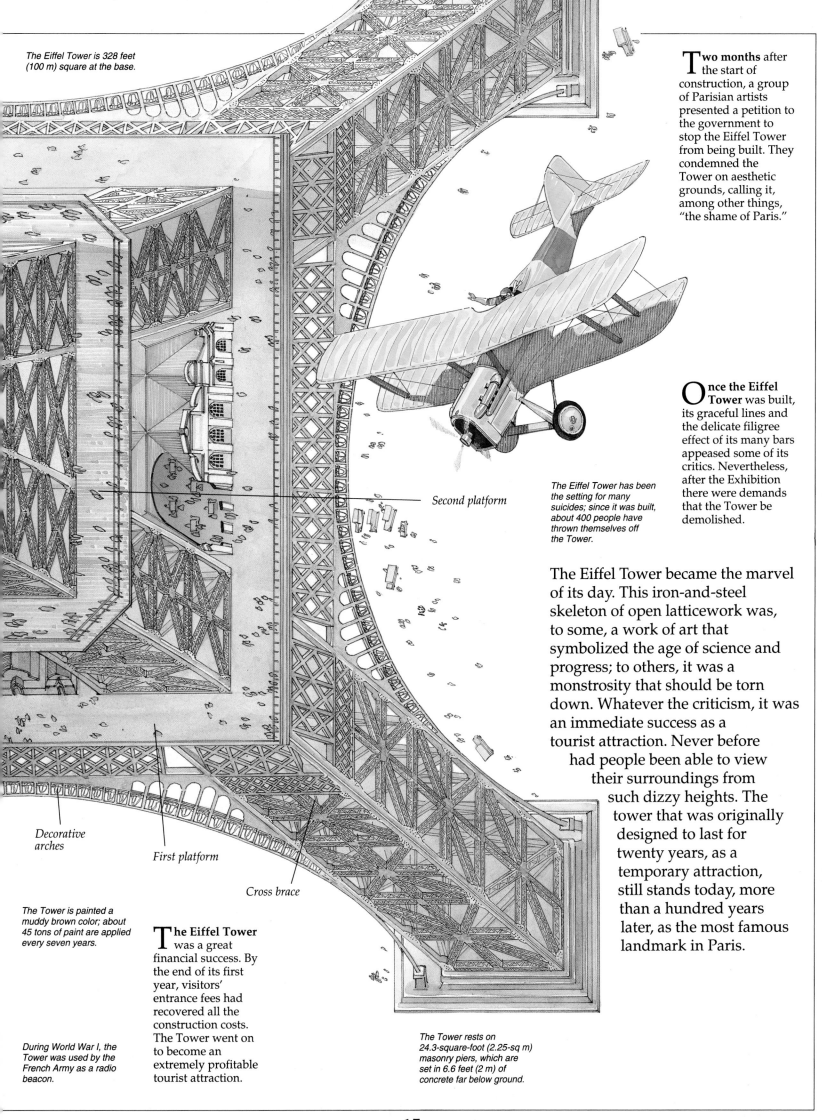

The Eiffel Tower is 328 feet (100 m) square at the base.

Two months after the start of construction, a group of Parisian artists presented a petition to the government to stop the Eiffel Tower from being built. They condemned the Tower on aesthetic grounds, calling it, among other things, "the shame of Paris."

Once the Eiffel Tower was built, its graceful lines and the delicate filigree effect of its many bars appeased some of its critics. Nevertheless, after the Exhibition there were demands that the Tower be demolished.

The Eiffel Tower has been the setting for many suicides; since it was built, about 400 people have thrown themselves off the Tower.

Second platform

The Eiffel Tower became the marvel of its day. This iron-and-steel skeleton of open latticework was, to some, a work of art that symbolized the age of science and progress; to others, it was a monstrosity that should be torn down. Whatever the criticism, it was an immediate success as a tourist attraction. Never before had people been able to view their surroundings from such dizzy heights. The tower that was originally designed to last for twenty years, as a temporary attraction, still stands today, more than a hundred years later, as the most famous landmark in Paris.

Decorative arches

First platform

Cross brace

The Tower is painted a muddy brown color; about 45 tons of paint are applied every seven years.

The Eiffel Tower was a great financial success. By the end of its first year, visitors' entrance fees had recovered all the construction costs. The Tower went on to become an extremely profitable tourist attraction.

During World War I, the Tower was used by the French Army as a radio beacon.

The Tower rests on 24.3-square-foot (2.25-sq m) masonry piers, which are set in 6.6 feet (2 m) of concrete far below ground.

BUILDING THE Eiffel Tower

The Eiffel Tower is taller than the combined height of St. Peter's Basilica (453 feet, or 138 m), the leaning Tower of Pisa (180 feet, or 55 m) and the Statue of Liberty (305 feet, or 93 m).

January 17, 1887	*June 16, 1887*	*April 7, 1888*	*August 21, 1888*	*March 15, 1889*	*May 5, 1889*
Laying the concrete foundations began in January 1887 and was finished in June 1887.	**T**he four legs were supported by scaffolding made of timber, and the components would be lifted by cranes.	**T**he first platform was finally completed in April 1888, and the lifting cranes were hoisted onto it.	**T**he second platform, which was to be built above the decorative arches, was finished by August 1888.	**A**fter an official ceremony the Eiffel Tower was finally opened to the general public on March 15, 1889.	**T**he third and final platform was added after the Tower had opened. It was completed in May 1889.

THE EIFFEL TOWER WAS MADE UP OF 18,038 wrought-iron components. Because wrought iron could not be welded, the parts had to be held together by rivets. The components were built off-site with extreme accuracy so that when they were hoisted into place, the holes in each part matched exactly. There were 5,300 drawings that specified the locations of the 2.5 million rivets.

The whole structure weighs over 9,000 tons and rests on a solid masonry foundation. The splayed legs and open latticework, which allow wind to pass through, mean that the Eiffel Tower can withstand the strongest of gales. The 1,050-foot (320-m) Tower becomes slightly taller on a hot summer's day, when it expands by as much as 6.7 inches (17 cm).

At the first platform, 187 feet (57 m) high, the 4 legs are linked by decorative arches. At the second platform, 377 feet (115 m) in height from the ground, the legs are brought completely together. The third platform is 906 feet (276 m) high. Above this is the lantern and final terrace.

Eiffel pioneered the use of the compressed-air caisson, which was a water-tight chamber. It was sunk into position and then compressed air was forced inside to keep soil and water from entering the bottom of the shaft and to provide air for the workers. As the soil was removed, the caisson sank. When it reached bedrock, the caisson was filled with concrete to become part of the foundation.

Alexandre-Gustave Eiffel succeeded in making his iron-and-steel structures appear so graceful that he became known as the Magician of Iron.

Caisson

Alexandre-Gustave Eiffel (1832–1923) was an engineer and an expert in building with wrought iron. When he began work on the Eiffel Tower he had already built numerous bridges, domes and roofs throughout the world using iron and steel. He had designed the huge locks for the Panama Canal as well as the steel framework of the Statue of Liberty.

When the Germans entered Paris during World War II, there was a "mysterious" problem with the elevators, which forced Hitler to climb the stairs to the top. When Paris was freed in 1944, the elevators were put right with the simple turn of a screw.

16

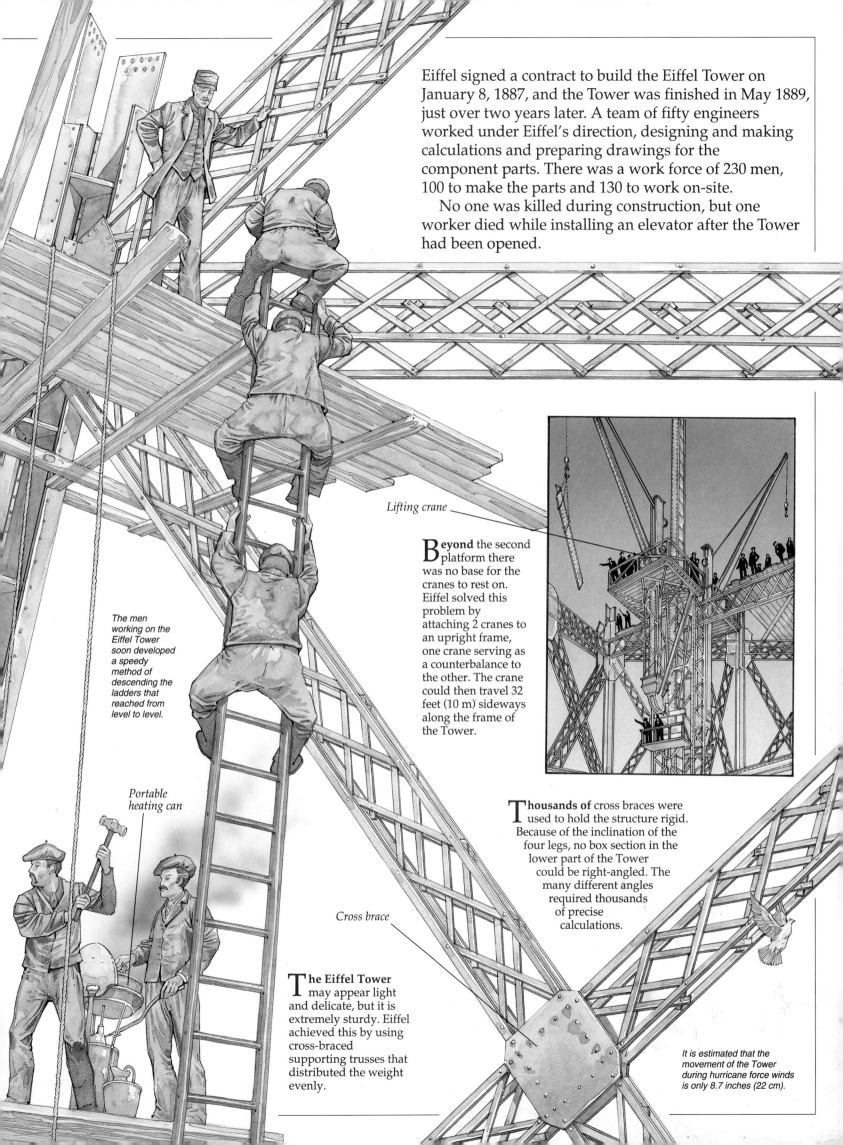

Eiffel signed a contract to build the Eiffel Tower on January 8, 1887, and the Tower was finished in May 1889, just over two years later. A team of fifty engineers worked under Eiffel's direction, designing and making calculations and preparing drawings for the component parts. There was a work force of 230 men, 100 to make the parts and 130 to work on-site.

No one was killed during construction, but one worker died while installing an elevator after the Tower had been opened.

Lifting crane

Beyond the second platform there was no base for the cranes to rest on. Eiffel solved this problem by attaching 2 cranes to an upright frame, one crane serving as a counterbalance to the other. The crane could then travel 32 feet (10 m) sideways along the frame of the Tower.

The men working on the Eiffel Tower soon developed a speedy method of descending the ladders that reached from level to level.

Portable heating can

Thousands of cross braces were used to hold the structure rigid. Because of the inclination of the four legs, no box section in the lower part of the Tower could be right-angled. The many different angles required thousands of precise calculations.

Cross brace

The Eiffel Tower may appear light and delicate, but it is extremely sturdy. Eiffel achieved this by using cross-braced supporting trusses that distributed the weight evenly.

It is estimated that the movement of the Tower during hurricane force winds is only 8.7 inches (22 cm).

TOWER BRIDGE

William George Armstrong (1810-1900), the inventor of the hydraulic system for Tower Bridge.

There were 4 coal-burning, double-furnace boilers. Each was more than 6.6 feet (2 m) in diameter and about 3.3 feet (10 m) long. Two were always in use to supply steam to the nearby pumping engine, which pumped water into the hydraulic system. The boilers used up about 20 tons of coal a week.

IN 1885, THE BRITISH PARLIAMENT decreed that another bridge should be built across the River Thames. It was to be London's last bridge before the open sea. However, there were certain requirements: architecturally, the bridge had to be in harmony with the nearby Norman castle, the Tower of London; structurally, it had to allow tall-masted ships through to the upper reaches of the Thames. The designers of Tower Bridge, as it became known, found ingenious solutions. A steel framework provided the necessary strength, while masonry cladding and elaborate decoration gave the bridge a medieval flavor. The two central drawbridges – or bascules – could be raised by hydraulic engines to leave a space through which the largest of ships could pass.

England

Accumulator

Engine house

Abutment tower

Pier

Steam pumping engine

The hydraulic system was simple but effective. A boiler supplied steam to the pumping engine, which pumped water under pressure to the six accumulators (two in the accumulator room close to the engine room and two in each tower). High-pressure water from the accumulators (or direct from the pumping engine) was conveyed along pipes to the bascule-drive machines in the tower piers. These machines used the power to turn a shaft with geared cogwheels at each end. The cogwheels meshed with immense toothed quadrants (quarter circles) connected to the bascules. As the quadrants turned, the bascules were raised or lowered.

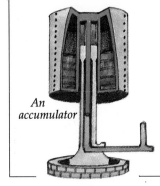

An accumulator

An accumulator was a 100-ton cylinder that stored and maintained the constant water pressure which was necessary to raise and lower the bascules.

The 2 shore spans, each approximately 269 feet (82 m) long, were suspended on steel tie rods from massive chains that ran from the tops of the main towers, and were anchored in huge blocks of concrete set into the riverbanks.

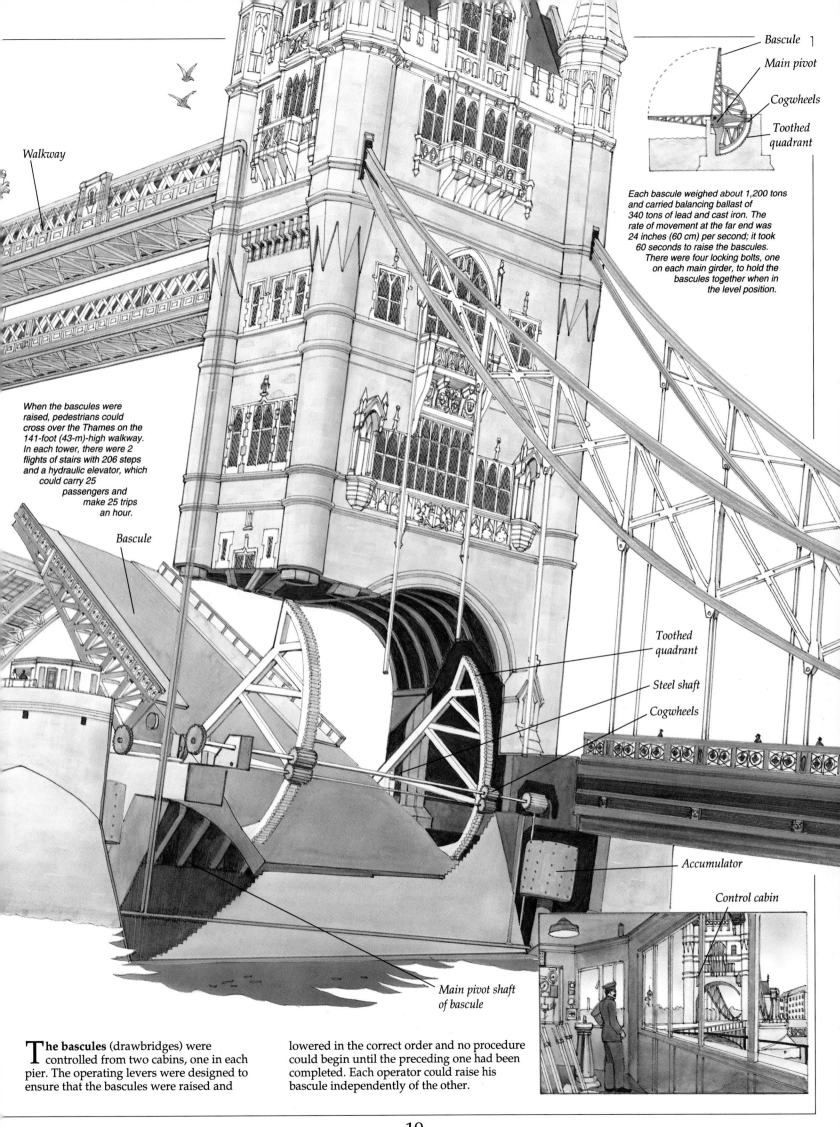

Walkway

Bascule

Main pivot

Cogwheels

Toothed quadrant

Each bascule weighed about 1,200 tons and carried balancing ballast of 340 tons of lead and cast iron. The rate of movement at the far end was 24 inches (60 cm) per second; it took 60 seconds to raise the bascules. There were four locking bolts, one on each main girder, to hold the bascules together when in the level position.

When the bascules were raised, pedestrians could cross over the Thames on the 141-foot (43-m)-high walkway. In each tower, there were 2 flights of stairs with 206 steps and a hydraulic elevator, which could carry 25 passengers and make 25 trips an hour.

Bascule

Toothed quadrant

Steel shaft

Cogwheels

Accumulator

Control cabin

Main pivot shaft of bascule

The bascules (drawbridges) were controlled from two cabins, one in each pier. The operating levers were designed to ensure that the bascules were raised and lowered in the correct order and no procedure could begin until the preceding one had been completed. Each operator could raise his bascule independently of the other.

BUILDING Tower Bridge

TOWER BRIDGE IN LONDON WAS equipped with a system of hydraulic engineering that used the power of pressurized water to operate its lifting machinery and to raise its passenger elevators to the high-level walkways. The machinery was installed by W. G. Armstrong's firm, as they were experts in hydraulic engineering. It was a masterpiece of design. All the machinery was duplicated; the second set was always ready to be used as a backup if needed. But there was ample power even at the busiest of times and the service was so faultless that this second set was never called into action. For over eighty years Tower Bridge was operated by hydraulic power. Armstrong's original machinery was modernized in the early 1970s.

Horace Jones (1819–1897), the chief architect for the city of London, designed Tower Bridge with the assistance of John Wolfe Barry. Jones died in 1887 before even the foundations were finished.

John Wolfe Barry (1837–1918), Britain's leading engineer, refined Horace Jones's bascule idea of a lifting central span. Barry assumed responsibility for building the bridge after the death of Horace Jones.

George Daniel Stevenson (1846–1918), Horace Jones's assistant, became the architectural consultant after Jones's death. Stevenson was responsible for the final architectural design of Tower Bridge.

In Horace Jones's original design, the arches did not allow the bascules to open fully. This narrowed the space through which tall-masted ships would be able to pass.

Brickwork exterior

Chains to raise the bascule

Arched girder

Bascule

Piers under construction showing the timber staging that held the large cranes.

The foundations for the 2 tower piers were dug out by men working inside caissons, open-ended boxes made of wrought iron, with sharp edges at the bottom that sank into the riverbed. Once the excavation was completed the area was filled with concrete to form the pier foundation.

In 1856, an English inventor, Henry Bessemer, introduced a new method of purifying iron, the result of which was the production of steel. Steel, because it is stronger and more durable, started to replace cast and wrought iron in bridge construction. The use of iron with steel meant that building became an exact science. At first, a number of bridges and buildings collapsed because builders did not know how to use the iron with the steel correctly. Engineers began to take over the design of the structural aspect of building, while architects dealt mainly with the appearance.

Timber roof with zinc covering

Cast-iron molding

Cast-iron tracery

Circular turrets containing steel columns

The steel framework for the towers was faced with gray granite and Portland stone (a type of limestone), and backed with brickwork. Before cladding was applied, the steel columns were treated to prevent rust.

Tower of London

Work started in 1886, and the Bridge was completed 8 years later, in 1894.

At the peak of the shipping era on the Thames, the bascules were raised up to 50 times a day.

The central section of the Bridge could be raised to leave a space over 197 feet (60 m) wide and 141 feet (43 m) high.

Any ship with a mast of 29.5 feet (9 m) or more could request that the Bridge be opened.

EMPIRE STATE BUILDING

Manhattan Island in New York City has the highest concentration of skyscrapers in the world.

New York

In 1929, the developers of the Empire State Building spent $16 million on the site for their proposed skyscraper.

THE SKYSCRAPER BECAME POSSIBLE with the development of the steel framing system and the invention of the electric elevator. The incentive to build higher came from the need to conserve valuable land space. At the turn of the century, Manhattan Island in New York City, a booming financial district with limited room for expansion, became the home for the world's largest office buildings. One of the most distinguished of Manhattan's skyscrapers was the Empire State Building, named after New York State – the Empire State. When completed in 1931, the Empire State Building was the tallest building in the world; it was 1,246 feet (380 m) high and had 102 stories.

The Empire State Building also holds the distinction of being the most quickly constructed skyscraper. Excavation of the foundations began in January 1930. By March 1930, work on the steel framework had begun; it was completed 23 weeks later. The building itself was finished on April 11, 1931. About three thousand workers were on the job daily. At one stage fourteen stories went up in ten days. The building was occupied four months ahead of schedule, but because of the Great Depression much of the office space remained empty until the outbreak of World War II in 1939.

The Empire State Building held the world record as the tallest skyscraper until 1972, when it was overtaken by the 1,375-foot (419-m)-high twin towers of the World Trade Center in Manhattan.

On October 24,1929, the Wall Street stock market crashed, triggering off the Great Depression.

While the stock market collapsed, the old Waldorf Astoria Hotel was demolished to clear the site.

More than 6,000 windows

740 tons of aluminium and stainless steel for the outer walls

1,172 miles (1,886 km) of wire for elevator cables

50 miles (80 km) of radiator pipe

70 miles (112 km) of water pipes

4,700 miles (7,600 km) of electrical wire

61,000 tons of steel for the frame

About 25,000 people work in the Empire State Building. It has 73 elevators that can move 10,000 people every hour. The 80th floor is reached in 56 seconds, the 102nd floor in 76 seconds.

196,000 cubic feet (5,600 cu.m) of limestone for the lower floors and walls

Lines for free food became a common sight. Construction costs dropped from $44 million to $25 million.

10 million bricks

Setback

Ground-floor entrance

1st level

The 223-foot (68-m)-high radio mast on the top of the Empire State Building brings its height to 1,472 feet (448.67 m) above street level.

Stepped plinth

Architects Richmond Shreve, William Lamb and Arthur Harmon changed their design sixteen times.

The Empire State Building has withstood many lightning strikes. It was once hit nine times in 20 minutes.

Radio tower

4th level

Ornamentation

Art deco shell forms round lantern

The top floor sways up to 3.3 feet (1 m) in a strong wind.

The observation floor, at a height of 1,050 feet (320 m), offers a view that on a clear day extends for 50 miles (80 km).

Because of wind currents around the Empire State Building, snow sweeps upwards instead of falling. The steel framework is so resilient that, in 1945, when a B25 bomber crashed into its side between the 78th and 79th floors, the stability of the building was not affected, although several offices were destroyed.

Offices

3rd level

Many of the workers on the Empire State Building were Mohawk Indians, as they seemed to lack a fear of heights. The riveters were paid just over $1.92 per hour, and were given a lunch of sandwiches and coffee for 40 cents. This was often sent up to them on the high beams using a bucket and pulleys.

Migrating birds became confused by the lighting on the radio mast and would fly into the building. The lights are now turned off during the migration seasons.

Once in position, the steel beam was first bolted into place and then the riveting gang made the connection permanent.

It was important to cap the rivet while it was still hot and malleable, so riveting crews had to work quickly. As it cooled, the length of the rivet shrank, thus tightening its bond.

Bucker-up

Riveter

Catcher

The driver on the other side of the hole, using a compressed-air hammer, smashed his end of the rivet into a wide cap, thereby bonding together the two sections of the framework. The riveter checked the work and supervised the gang.

Overseers used bells to direct the placement of the steel beams. The sound of the bells indicated to the cable machine operator, who was usually out of sight of the bell ringer, to raise or lower the beam into place. Sometimes a worker would ride on the beam, holding onto the cable and guiding the beam with his feet.

The catcher took the rivet in his tongs and jammed it into the hole. The bucker-up held the rivet in place with a heavy steel dolly bar powered by compressed air.

Riveting gangs were made up of five men – the heater, the catcher, the bucker-up, the riveter and the driver. There was also a young helper known as a punk.

The heater heated ten or more rivets on his forge until they were red-hot. Then, using tongs, he took a rivet out of the forge and tossed it to the catcher, who caught it in midair in his catching can.

Chrysler building

Driver

2nd level

Punk

Heater

To the high-iron workers, who stood on steel beams 102 stories high, the people walking the Manhattan streets below looked like tiny ants.

SKYSCRAPERS

The thirteenth-century skyline of the Italian city of Bologna was similar to that of modern Manhattan. The tall fortified homes served as protection when the city was at war.

THE DESIGN OF Manhattan's early skyscrapers was determined by the 1916 building code. When a building reached 125 feet (38 m) in height it had to be set back to be less than the width of the street it was on. At the thirtieth floor, it had to be set back again, making the floor size no more than one quarter of the size of the land on which the building stood. The result was the stepped characteristic of the Empire State and Chrysler Buildings.

Stainless-steel spire

Chevron pattern

The Chrysler Building in New York was designed by the architect William Van Alen and completed in 1930. From ground level to the top of the spire, it stood at 319 metres high, and was the tallest building in the world, only to be beaten into second place the following year by the Empire State Building. The upper part of the building is decorated with the Chrysler car logo and a frieze of silver-colored hubcaps. Eagles modeled on the Chrysler car's chrome hood ornament are on the four corners of the sixty-first floor.

Hubcab motif

Stainless-steel eagles modeled on the Chrysler car's hood ornament

The Flatiron Building in New York (shown above left) was shaped to fit a triangular site, and rose to a height of 299 feet (91 m). When completed in 1903, it was the tallest building in the world. The exterior was clad with decorative terra-cotta stonework (above).

The Woolworth Building held the record as the tallest office building from 1913 to 1930.

An image of the Woolworth Building's architect, Cass Gilbert, holding his creation (shown left), was carved into the lobby ceiling.

Almost the entire surface of the Woolworth Building in New York is covered in terra-cotta ornamentation. About 16 million bricks were placed between the terra-cotta and the steel framework. The terra-cotta blocks were then hooked onto the brick backing and cemented into place. The Woolworth Building, at 791 feet (241 m) high, was the world's tallest building when it was erected in 1913. Its 25-story tower rests on a 35-story base. The tower rises in three stages, and is crowned with a decorative peak.

Set back from street baseline

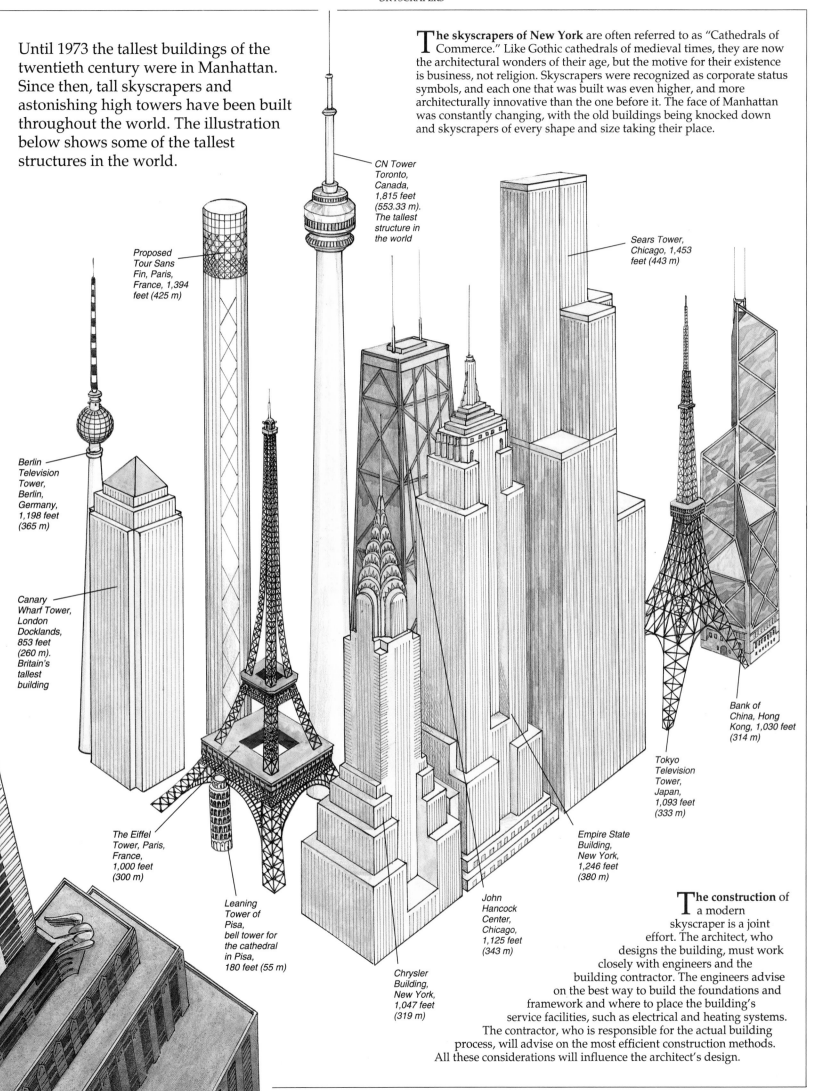

Until 1973 the tallest buildings of the twentieth century were in Manhattan. Since then, tall skyscrapers and astonishing high towers have been built throughout the world. The illustration below shows some of the tallest structures in the world.

The skyscrapers of New York are often referred to as "Cathedrals of Commerce." Like Gothic cathedrals of medieval times, they are now the architectural wonders of their age, but the motive for their existence is business, not religion. Skyscrapers were recognized as corporate status symbols, and each one that was built was even higher, and more architecturally innovative than the one before it. The face of Manhattan was constantly changing, with the old buildings being knocked down and skyscrapers of every shape and size taking their place.

CN Tower Toronto, Canada, 1,815 feet (553.33 m). The tallest structure in the world

Proposed Tour Sans Fin, Paris, France, 1,394 feet (425 m)

Sears Tower, Chicago, 1,453 feet (443 m)

Berlin Television Tower, Berlin, Germany, 1,198 feet (365 m)

Canary Wharf Tower, London Docklands, 853 feet (260 m). Britain's tallest building

The Eiffel Tower, Paris, France, 1,000 feet (300 m)

Leaning Tower of Pisa, bell tower for the cathedral in Pisa, 180 feet (55 m)

Chrysler Building, New York, 1,047 feet (319 m)

John Hancock Center, Chicago, 1,125 feet (343 m)

Empire State Building, New York, 1,246 feet (380 m)

Bank of China, Hong Kong, 1,030 feet (314 m)

Tokyo Television Tower, Japan, 1,093 feet (333 m)

The construction of a modern skyscraper is a joint effort. The architect, who designs the building, must work closely with engineers and the building contractor. The engineers advise on the best way to build the foundations and framework and where to place the building's service facilities, such as electrical and heating systems. The contractor, who is responsible for the actual building process, will advise on the most efficient construction methods. All these considerations will influence the architect's design.

SAGRADA FAMILIA

THE CHURCH OF THE SAGRADA FAMILIA in Barcelona was built in honor of the Holy Family – Jesus, Mary and Joseph. Its leaning towers, warped surfaces and lavish decorations make it one of the most unusual buildings of the modern world. Its originality can be credited to one man alone – Antoni Gaudí, whose involvement began in 1883 when the church's original architect, Francisco de Villar, resigned. Gaudí was already well known for his extraordinary buildings, and when he took over the Sagrada Familia he drastically altered the original plan for the church. Gaudí wanted people to be able to "read" the outside of his church like a huge book. He was fascinated by symbolism, shapes and surfaces, and looked to the sea, plants and rock formations for his inspiration. In nature he found the flowing lines and the irregular shapes that were to become his "signature," and these were the forms that he used to tell the story of the Holy Family and the birth and death of Christ.

Gaudí's original plan for the church had twelve bell towers – four for each of the three façades of the building. These towers were to represent the twelve apostles. The center of the church symbolized the body of Christ, and the main spire, which is crowned with a cross, represented Christ as the head of the Church and the savior of mankind.

Gaudí lived to see only part of his masterpiece completed, and the Sagrada Familia remains unfinished.

At the time of Gaudí's death, only three of the four eastern towers had been finished.

Spain

St. Matthias

St. Thaddeus

St. Simon

St. Barnabas

Mosaic crosses

The tops of the towers are decorated with colored mosaics and pearl shapes.

The four bell towers on the eastern side of the church are over 302 feet (92 m) tall and have the words "Sanctus, sanctus, sanctus" carved into them. The tops of the bell towers have the words "Hosanna in Excelsis" placed around their spires.

The bell towers are dedicated from left to right to the apostles Barnabas, Simon, Thaddeus and Matthias.

St. Barnabas was the only tower to be completed in Gaudí's lifetime.

"Hosanna in Excelsis"

The main tower of the Sagrada Familia was to be illuminated to symbolize Christ as the light of the world.

The words "Sanctus, sanctus, sanctus," which are carved into the towers in a stepped design, lead the eyes towards heaven.

The bell towers lean inwards.

The stone cypress tree above the Portal of Love symbolizes immortality.

Hollow towers

Cypress tree

Parabolic arches

East Façade

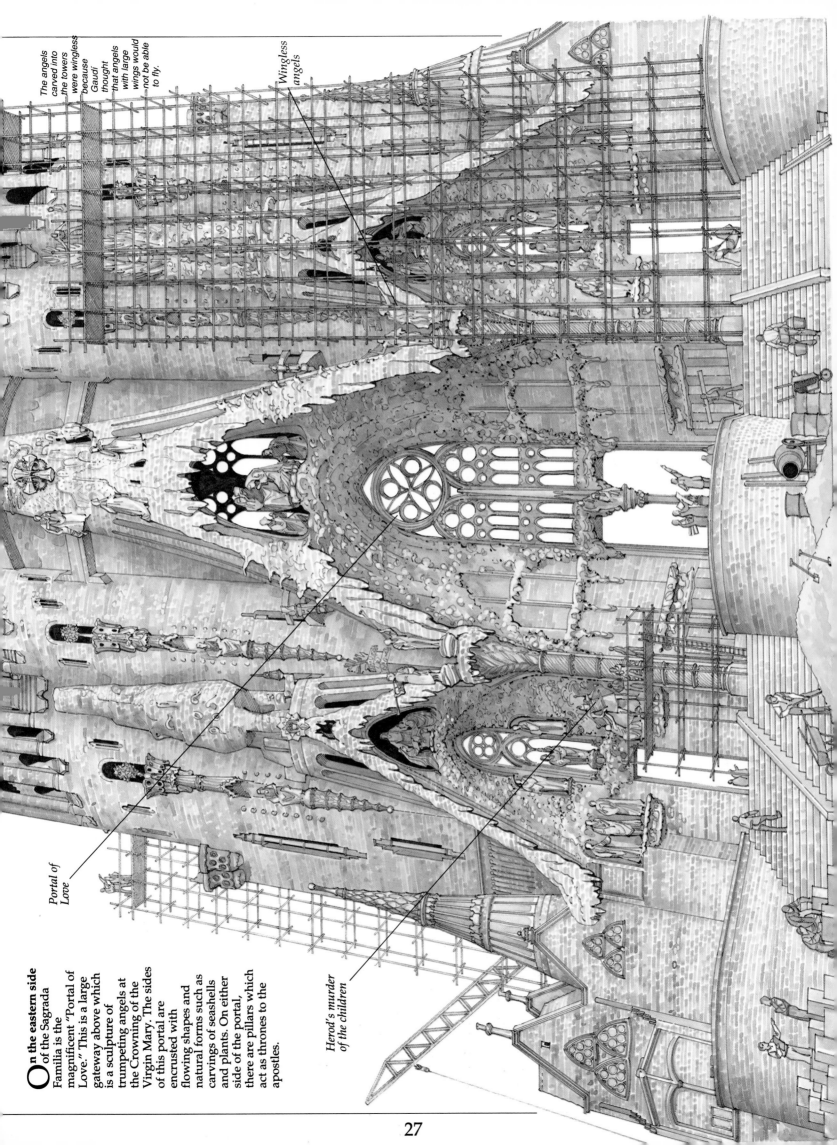

On the eastern side of the Sagrada Familia is the magnificent "Portal of Love." This is a large gateway above which is a sculpture of trumpeting angels at the Crowning of the Virgin Mary. The sides of this portal are encrusted with flowing shapes and natural forms such as carvings of seashells and plants. On either side of the portal, there are pillars which act as thrones to the apostles.

The angels carved into the towers were wingless because Gaudí thought that angels with large wings would not be able to fly.

Wingless angels

Portal of Love

Herod's murder of the children

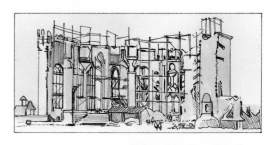

The Sagrada Familia was started in 1882 in Barcelona, Spain, and was dedicated to Jesus, Mary, and Joseph – the Holy Family.

Antoni Gaudí was only 31 years old when he designed the Sagrada Familia. He died in 1926, aged 74.

The 1889 view (above) of the Sagrada Familia shows how Gaudí's plan started to take shape. It took 6 years to reach the stage shown on the right.

By 1895 Gaudí had started the east façade. The people of Barcelona wanted him to build the west façade first because it faced the city. But Gaudí argued that because the east façade represented the birth of Christ, it should be built before the west, which was to represent the death of Christ.

Construction of the Sagrada Familia continues today. This is a view of the interior of the church.

This is what the Sagrada Familia would look like if it had been finished. The areas in pink are not yet completed.

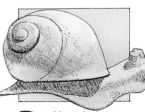

Gaudí copied nature for many of his decorations. Here is a sculpture of a snail that adorns the Sagrada Familia.

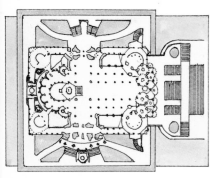

Above: Gaudí's plan for the Sagrada Familia.

Below: One of the towers of the Nativity façade.

Gaudí lived in a small workshop on the site of the Sagrada Familia and was involved in every aspect of its design and engineering.

MODERN CATHEDRALS

AT THE TIME OF GAUDI'S DEATH only the apse walls and the Nativity façade of the Sagrada Familia had been completed. Gaudí's plan was for three façades representing Christ's birth, death, and resurrection. Each façade was to have three portals, representing Love, Faith and Hope, and four towers 328 feet (100 m) high, making a total of twelve towers to represent the twelve Apostles. Above the 328-foot (100-m)-long nave, Gaudí planned to build taller towers, as high as 558 feet (170 m), around a central one that represented Christ. Work on the Sagrada Familia has continued for over one hundred years except for a long break from 1936, when the Spanish Civil War broke out, until 1952. But the church, as Gaudí envisaged it, is still far from complete. If it is ever finished, the Sagrada Familia will be the biggest church in the world.

The Cathedral Church of St. John the Divine in New York City was another church that was never finished. It was started in 1892 and building continued until 1941, when the United States entered World War II. Work was started again in 1972, and today the Cathedral is still only two-thirds complete. The Basilica of Our Lady of Peace in the Ivory Coast, Africa, was modeled on St. Peter's in Rome, but has surpassed it as the largest church. The dome of Our Lady of Peace is lower, but the crown and golden cross on top give it a height of 518 feet (158 m), which is 69 feet (21 m) higher than St. Peter's. Our Lady of Peace is 633 feet (193 m) long, 20 feet (6 m) longer than St. Peter's.

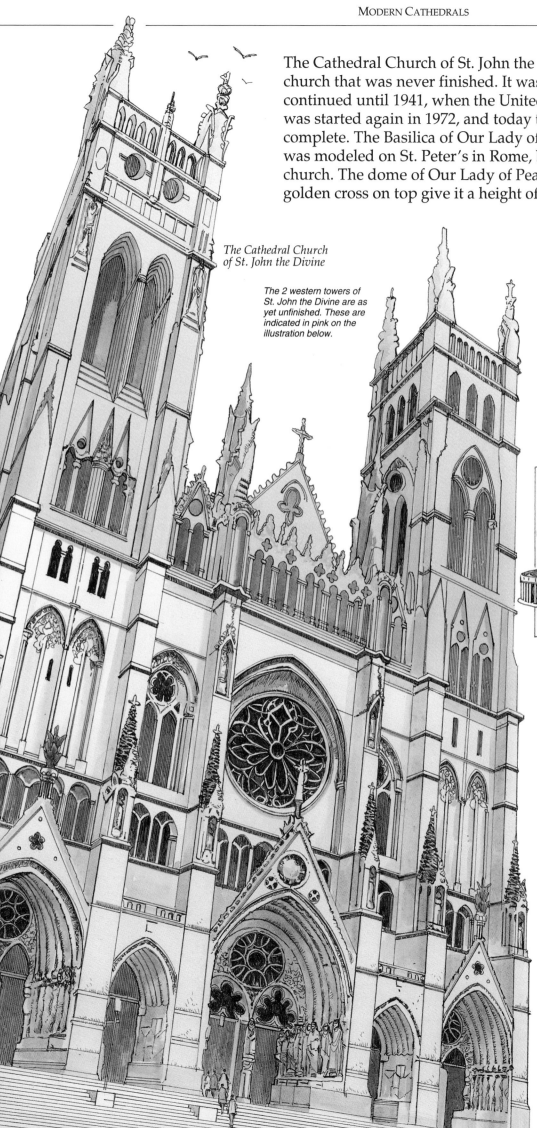

The Cathedral Church of St. John the Divine

The 2 western towers of St. John the Divine are as yet unfinished. These are indicated in pink on the illustration below.

The **Cathedral Church** of St. John the Divine in New York is built in the Gothic style of the great cathedrals of the Middle Ages. Only traditional building materials – stone, brick and tiles – have been used, except for the steel beam that supports the concrete roof. All the workers were hired from the local community and trained and supervised by master stonemasons.

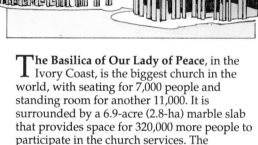

The Basilica of Our Lady of Peace

The **Basilica of Our Lady of Peace**, in the Ivory Coast, is the biggest church in the world, with seating for 7,000 people and standing room for another 11,000. It is surrounded by a 6.9-acre (2.8-ha) marble slab that provides space for 320,000 more people to participate in the church services. The church was started in 1987 and completed in less than 3 years.

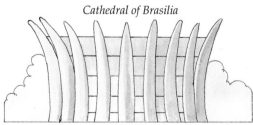

Cathedral of Brasilia

In the **1950s**, the city of Brasilia was built as the new capital of Brazil. Set among the futuristic government buildings is Brasilia's Cathedral, with its 16 sickle-shaped concrete ribs rising from a concrete ring 200 feet (60 m) in diameter. The ribs come together at the roof, 100 feet (30 m) high. The areas between the ribs are glassed in. The floor of the church is about 10 feet (3 m) below ground level and is reached by a ramp.

POMPIDOU CENTER

THE USE OF STEEL, CONCRETE, AND GLASS, in conjunction with sophisticated technology to control the heating, lighting, and ventilation inside buildings, has enabled higher and larger structures to be built. In the 1960s and 1970s, when the emphasis was on straight lines, rectangular shapes, and unadorned surfaces, architecture seemed to lack flair and imagination. Big buildings became big boxes. But in recent years there has been a move back to designing buildings that have irregular outlines and interesting decorative features. Rather than looking to past architectural traditions for inspiration, one new trend is to use the building's own structural and service technologies as forms of decoration. Structural cross beams and service mechanisms such as ventilation shafts are no longer hidden away but are boldly displayed on the outside of the building.

Because technology has become a prominent component of the building's design, this style of architecture is often referred to as high-tech.

One of the first and most famous high-tech buildings is the Pompidou Center in Paris, designed by Richard Rogers and Renzo Piano and built between 1971 and 1977. The architects turned the building inside out, with all the service mechanisms on the outside, forming part of the building's decoration.

Architects were able to design large areas of open space inside for art galleries, a library and an experimental music workshop. Each floor is the size of 2 soccer fields. Movable partitions mean that the interior space can be changed to accommodate a variety of uses.

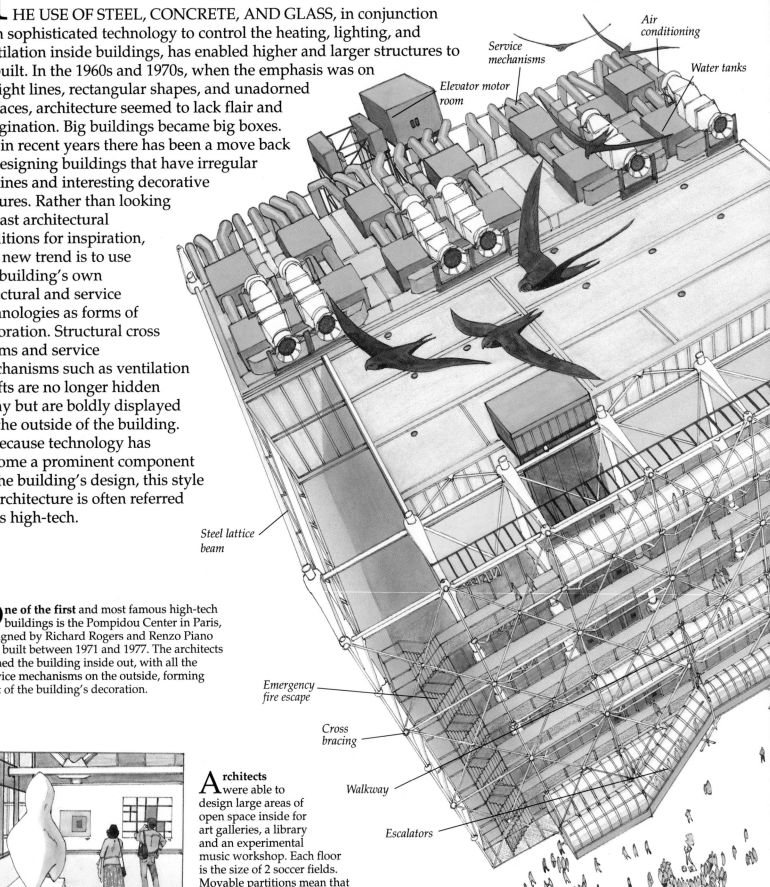

The Pompidou Center for Art and Culture was built in the Place Beaubourg in Paris, France.

France

Cooling tower

Air conditioning

Service mechanisms

Water tanks

Elevator motor room

Steel lattice beam

Emergency fire escape

Cross bracing

Walkway

Escalators

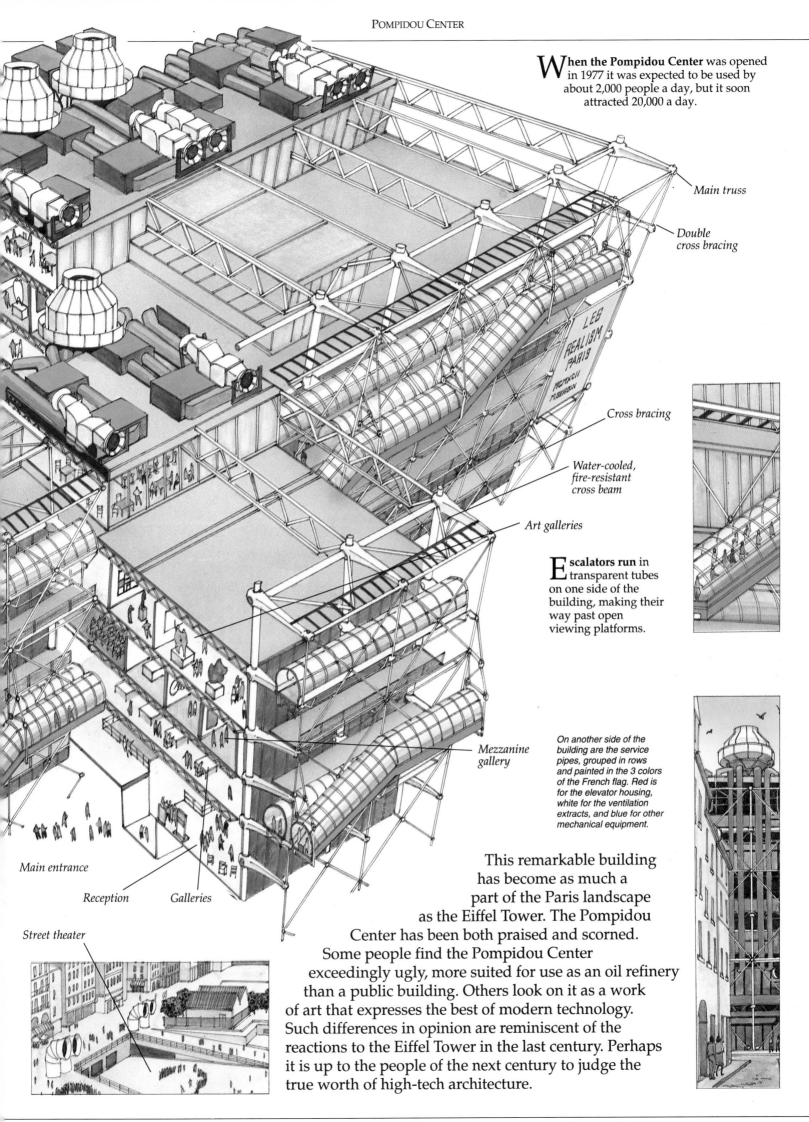

When the **Pompidou Center** was opened in 1977 it was expected to be used by about 2,000 people a day, but it soon attracted 20,000 a day.

Main truss

Double cross bracing

Cross bracing

Water-cooled, fire-resistant cross beam

Art galleries

Escalators run in transparent tubes on one side of the building, making their way past open viewing platforms.

Mezzanine gallery

On another side of the building are the service pipes, grouped in rows and painted in the 3 colors of the French flag. Red is for the elevator housing, white for the ventilation extracts, and blue for other mechanical equipment.

Main entrance

Reception   Galleries

Street theater

This remarkable building has become as much a part of the Paris landscape as the Eiffel Tower. The Pompidou Center has been both praised and scorned. Some people find the Pompidou Center exceedingly ugly, more suited for use as an oil refinery than a public building. Others look on it as a work of art that expresses the best of modern technology. Such differences in opinion are reminiscent of the reactions to the Eiffel Tower in the last century. Perhaps it is up to the people of the next century to judge the true worth of high-tech architecture.

HIGH-TECH BUILDINGS

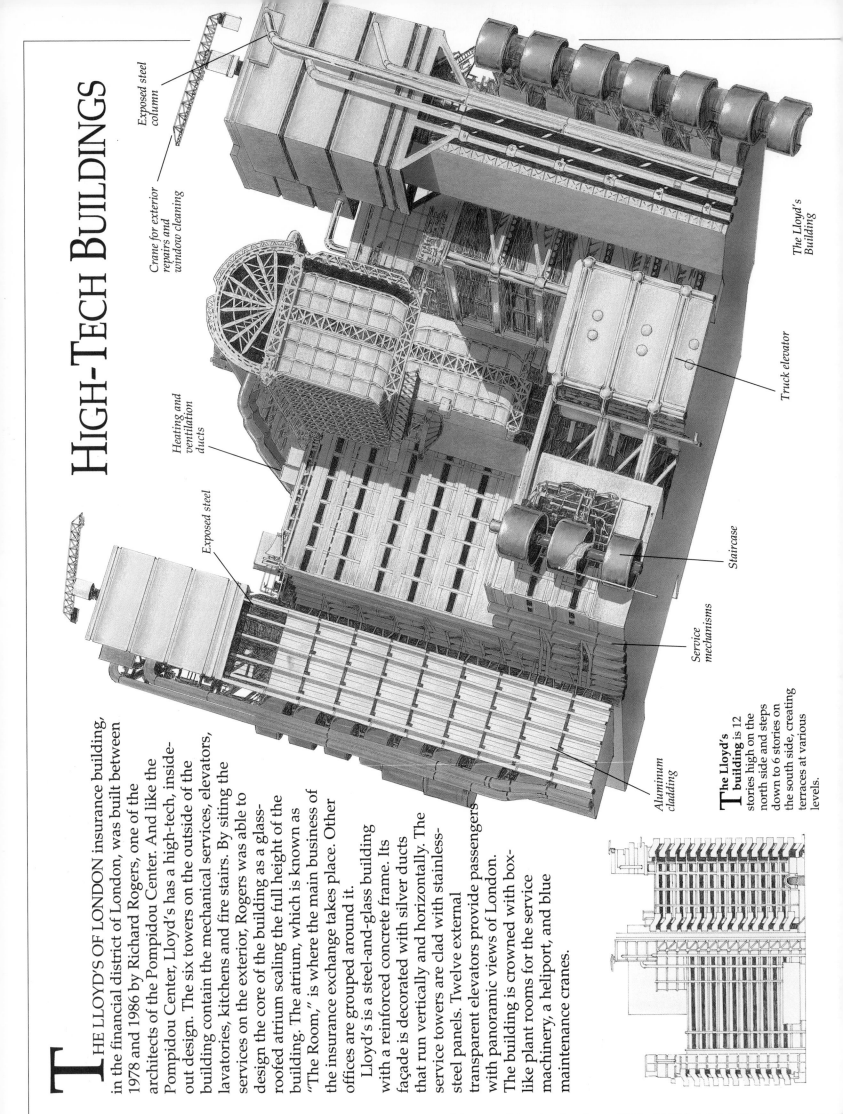

THE LLOYD'S OF LONDON insurance building, in the financial district of London, was built between 1978 and 1986 by Richard Rogers, one of the architects of the Pompidou Center. And like the Pompidou Center, Lloyd's has a high-tech, inside-out design. The six towers on the outside of the building contain the mechanical services, elevators, lavatories, kitchens and fire stairs. By siting the services on the exterior, Rogers was able to design the core of the building as a glass-roofed atrium scaling the full height of the building. The atrium, which is known as "The Room," is where the main business of the insurance exchange takes place. Other offices are grouped around it.

Lloyd's is a steel-and-glass building with a reinforced concrete frame. Its façade is decorated with silver ducts that run vertically and horizontally. The service towers are clad with stainless-steel panels. Twelve external transparent elevators provide passengers with panoramic views of London. The building is crowned with box-like plant rooms for the service machinery, a heliport, and blue maintenance cranes.

Exposed steel column

Crane for exterior repairs and window cleaning

Heating and ventilation ducts

Exposed steel

The Lloyd's Building

Truck elevator

Staircase

Service mechanisms

Aluminum cladding

The Lloyd's building is 12 stories high on the north side and steps down to 6 stories on the south side, creating terraces at various levels.

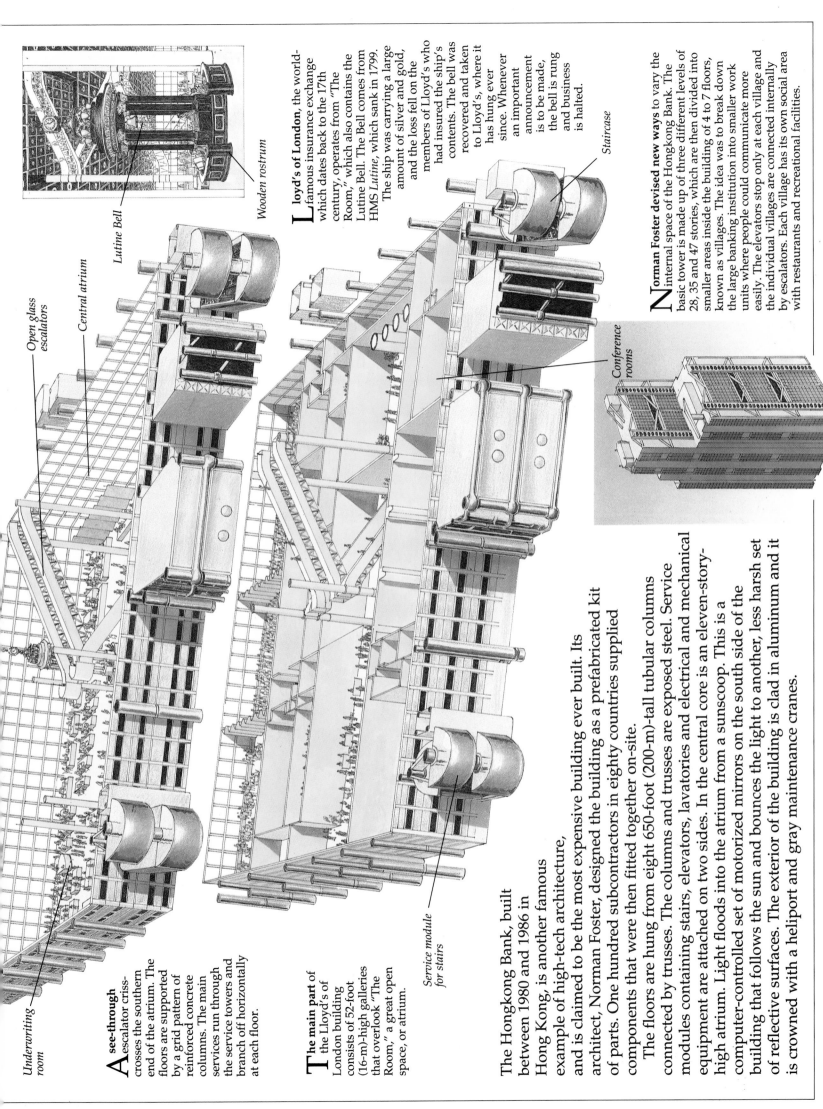

Underwriting room

Open glass escalators

Central atrium

Lutine Bell

Wooden rostrum

Staircase

Service module for stairs

Conference rooms

A see-through escalator crisscrosses the southern end of the atrium. The floors are supported by a grid pattern of reinforced concrete columns. The main services run through the service towers and branch off horizontally at each floor.

The main part of the Lloyd's of London building consists of 52-foot (16-m)-high galleries that overlook "The Room," a great open space, or atrium.

Lloyd's of London, the world-famous insurance exchange which dates back to the 17th century, operates from "The Room," which also contains the Lutine Bell. The Bell comes from HMS *Lutine,* which sank in 1799. The ship was carrying a large amount of silver and gold, and the loss fell on the members of Lloyd's who had insured the ship's contents. The bell was recovered and taken to Lloyd's, where it has hung ever since. Whenever an important announcement is to be made, the bell is rung and business is halted.

Norman Foster devised new ways to vary the internal space of the Hongkong Bank. The basic tower is made up of three different levels of 28, 35 and 47 stories, which are then divided into smaller areas inside the building of 4 to 7 floors, known as villages. The idea was to break down the large banking institution into smaller work units where people could communicate more easily. The elevators stop only at each village and the individual villages are connected internally by escalators. Each village has its own social area with restaurants and recreational facilities.

The Hongkong Bank, built between 1980 and 1986 in Hong Kong, is another famous example of high-tech architecture, and is claimed to be the most expensive building ever built. Its architect, Norman Foster, designed the building as a prefabricated kit of parts. One hundred subcontractors in eighty countries supplied components that were then fitted together on-site.

The floors are hung from eight 650-foot (200-m)-tall tubular columns connected by trusses. The columns and trusses are exposed steel. Service modules containing stairs, elevators, lavatories and electrical and mechanical equipment are attached on two sides. In the central core is an eleven-story-high atrium. Light floods into the atrium from a sunscoop. This is a computer-controlled set of motorized mirrors on the south side of the building that follows the sun and bounces the light to another, less harsh set of reflective surfaces. The exterior of the building is clad in aluminum and it is crowned with a heliport and gray maintenance cranes.

SYDNEY OPERA HOUSE

The Sydney Opera House is set on a magnificent site on Bennelong Point in Sydney Harbor, Australia.

THE USE OF REINFORCED CONCRETE as a building material opened up new possibilities in design. The steel rods or meshes that are embedded in the concrete make it stronger; they also give the concrete the ability to withstand bending and stretching forces caused by wind and heat. This has enabled architects to create daring structures with curving walls and immense roofs in the form of thin covering shells. Concrete has been used in a spectacular way in the construction of the sail-like shells of the Sydney Opera House in Australia.

The amber-colored glass walls that fill the open ends of the shells are supported by vertical steel bars and horizontal bronze glazing bars. There are 2,000 panes of glass and over 700 different shapes varying in size from about 10.8 feet (1 m) square to 13 feet (9 m) by 8 feet (2.5 m).

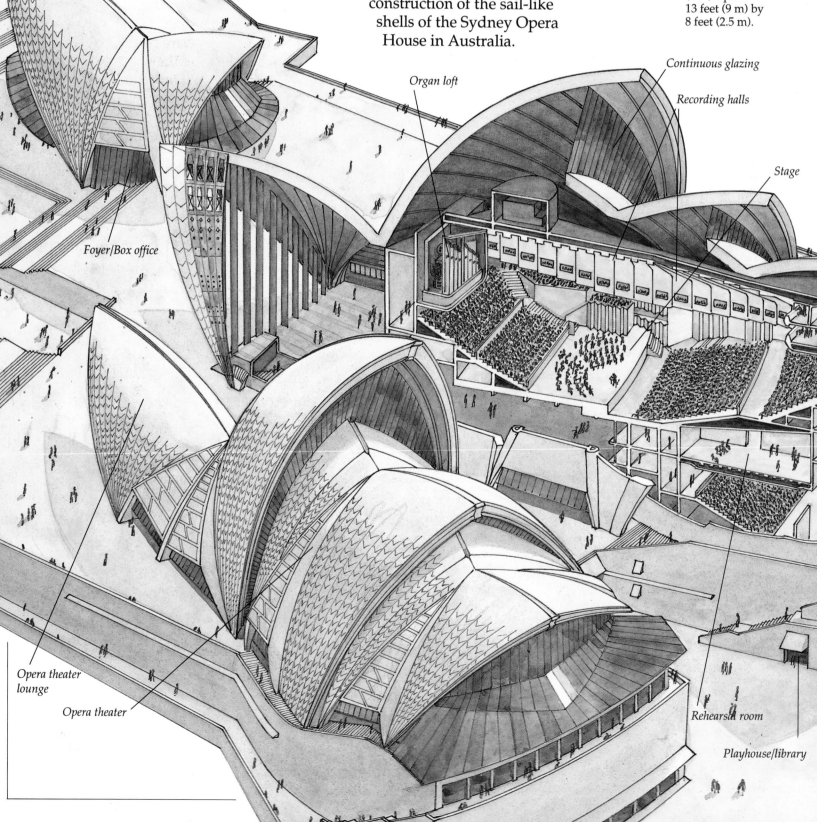

Organ loft

Continuous glazing

Recording halls

Stage

Foyer/Box office

Opera theater lounge

Opera theater

Rehearsal room

Playhouse/library

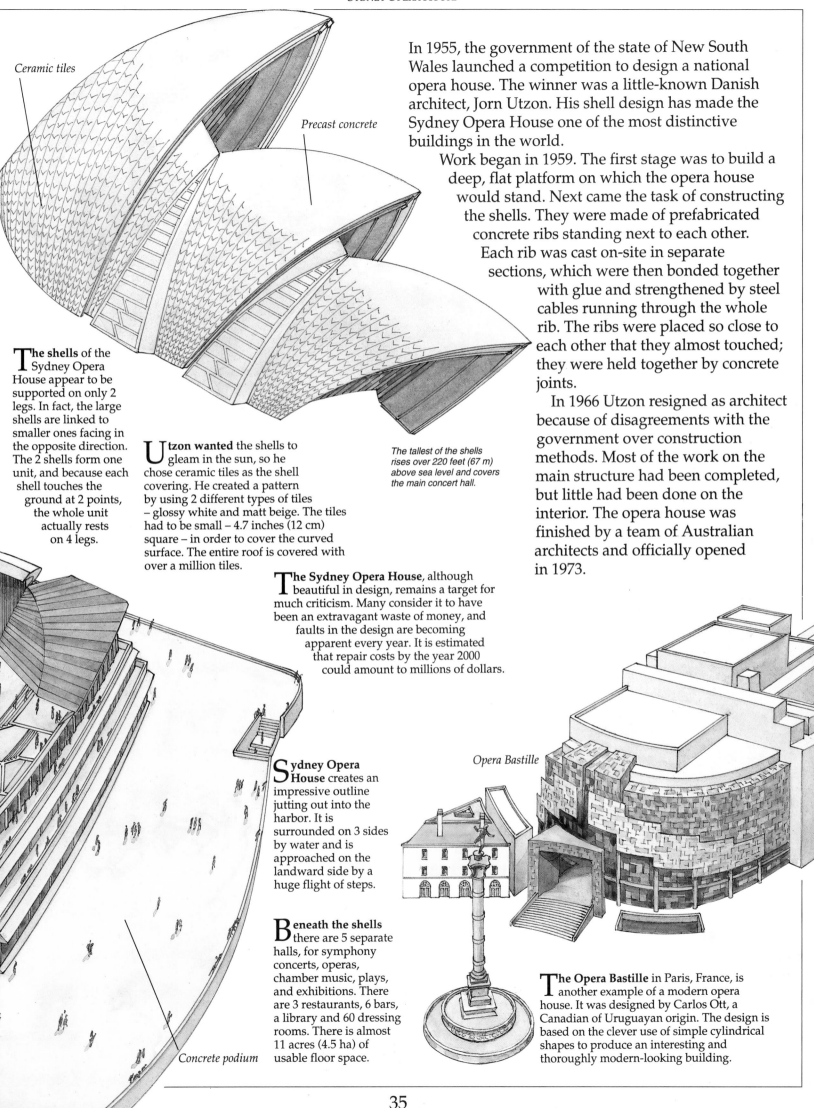

Ceramic tiles

Precast concrete

In 1955, the government of the state of New South Wales launched a competition to design a national opera house. The winner was a little-known Danish architect, Jorn Utzon. His shell design has made the Sydney Opera House one of the most distinctive buildings in the world.

Work began in 1959. The first stage was to build a deep, flat platform on which the opera house would stand. Next came the task of constructing the shells. They were made of prefabricated concrete ribs standing next to each other. Each rib was cast on-site in separate sections, which were then bonded together with glue and strengthened by steel cables running through the whole rib. The ribs were placed so close to each other that they almost touched; they were held together by concrete joints.

In 1966 Utzon resigned as architect because of disagreements with the government over construction methods. Most of the work on the main structure had been completed, but little had been done on the interior. The opera house was finished by a team of Australian architects and officially opened in 1973.

The shells of the Sydney Opera House appear to be supported on only 2 legs. In fact, the large shells are linked to smaller ones facing in the opposite direction. The 2 shells form one unit, and because each shell touches the ground at 2 points, the whole unit actually rests on 4 legs.

Utzon wanted the shells to gleam in the sun, so he chose ceramic tiles as the shell covering. He created a pattern by using 2 different types of tiles – glossy white and matt beige. The tiles had to be small – 4.7 inches (12 cm) square – in order to cover the curved surface. The entire roof is covered with over a million tiles.

The tallest of the shells rises over 220 feet (67 m) above sea level and covers the main concert hall.

The Sydney Opera House, although beautiful in design, remains a target for much criticism. Many consider it to have been an extravagant waste of money, and faults in the design are becoming apparent every year. It is estimated that repair costs by the year 2000 could amount to millions of dollars.

Sydney Opera House creates an impressive outline jutting out into the harbor. It is surrounded on 3 sides by water and is approached on the landward side by a huge flight of steps.

Beneath the shells there are 5 separate halls, for symphony concerts, operas, chamber music, plays, and exhibitions. There are 3 restaurants, 6 bars, a library and 60 dressing rooms. There is almost 11 acres (4.5 ha) of usable floor space.

Concrete podium

Opera Bastille

The Opera Bastille in Paris, France, is another example of a modern opera house. It was designed by Carlos Ott, a Canadian of Uruguayan origin. The design is based on the clever use of simple cylindrical shapes to produce an interesting and thoroughly modern-looking building.

FANTASTIC STRUCTURES

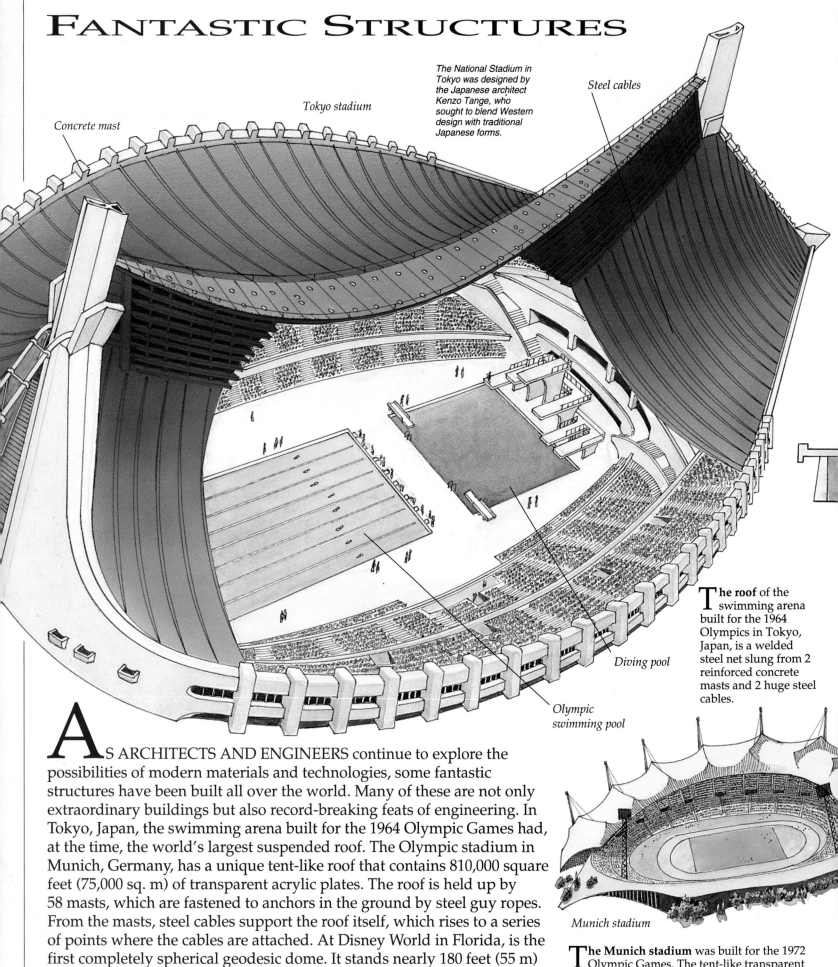

Tokyo stadium

The National Stadium in Tokyo was designed by the Japanese architect Kenzo Tange, who sought to blend Western design with traditional Japanese forms.

Concrete mast

Steel cables

Diving pool

Olympic swimming pool

The roof of the swimming arena built for the 1964 Olympics in Tokyo, Japan, is a welded steel net slung from 2 reinforced concrete masts and 2 huge steel cables.

Munich stadium

The Munich stadium was built for the 1972 Olympic Games. The tent-like transparent acrylic roof covers just over half the Olympic stadium; the other half is uncovered. The stadium is built of reinforced concrete and at its highest point rises to 108 feet (33 m).

AS ARCHITECTS AND ENGINEERS continue to explore the possibilities of modern materials and technologies, some fantastic structures have been built all over the world. Many of these are not only extraordinary buildings but also record-breaking feats of engineering. In Tokyo, Japan, the swimming arena built for the 1964 Olympic Games had, at the time, the world's largest suspended roof. The Olympic stadium in Munich, Germany, has a unique tent-like roof that contains 810,000 square feet (75,000 sq. m) of transparent acrylic plates. The roof is held up by 58 masts, which are fastened to anchors in the ground by steel guy ropes. From the masts, steel cables support the roof itself, which rises to a series of points where the cables are attached. At Disney World in Florida, is the first completely spherical geodesic dome. It stands nearly 180 feet (55 m) high and has a diameter of 164 feet (50 m). The Geodesic Golfball, as it is called, rests on three pairs of steel legs 33 feet (10 m) wide and rises almost 16 feet (5 m) above the ground.

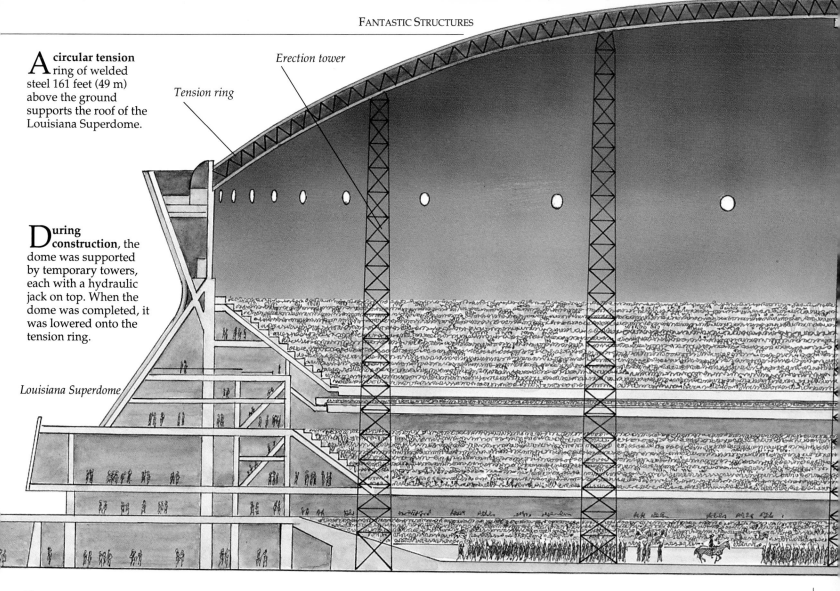

A circular tension ring of welded steel 161 feet (49 m) above the ground supports the roof of the Louisiana Superdome.

Erection tower

Tension ring

During construction, the dome was supported by temporary towers, each with a hydraulic jack on top. When the dome was completed, it was lowered onto the tension ring.

Louisiana Superdome

Inside Biosphere II in Arizona (below) is a 5-story building, a rain forest, a desert, an ocean with coral reef and tides, a savannah region and a selection of animals.

The Louisiana Superdome (above), opened in 1975, is the world's largest indoor stadium. The domed roof covers an area of almost 10 acres (4 ha). The seating capacity is 78,000.

The Geodesic Golfball at Disney World in Florida is made of a steel framework clad with nearly 1,000 triangular aluminum panels.

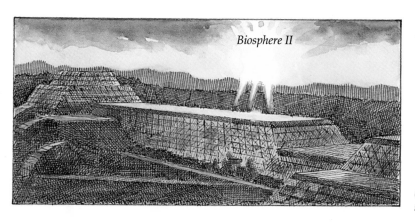

Biosphere II

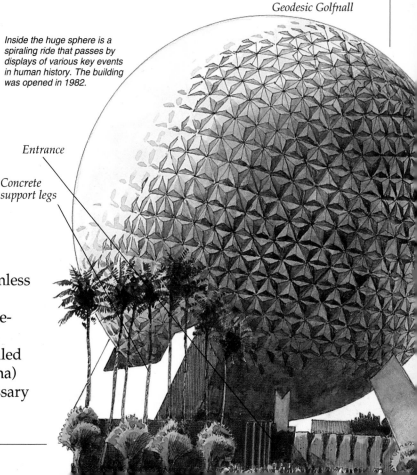

Geodesic Golfnall

Inside the huge sphere is a spiraling ride that passes by displays of various key events in human history. The building was opened in 1982.

Entrance

Concrete support legs

The dome covering the Louisiana Superdome in New Orleans is the largest in the world. It is 679 feet (207 m) in diameter and rises in the center to a height of 272 feet (83 m). The dome's steel framework is covered with a seamless skin of white plastic.

Biosphere II in America's Arizona Desert is the first large-scale attempt to simulate the environment and ecological behavior of planet Earth (Biosphere I). This completely sealed structure of steel and glass covers an area of 3.2 acres (1.3 ha) and attempted to provide all the food, water, and air necessary for the eight people who lived in it for two years.

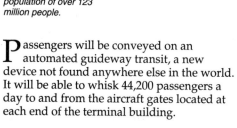

Japan

Japan is an island group in East Asia. It has a total population of over 123 million people.

A split-level truss bridge 2.3 miles (3.75 km) long, which will carry both motor vehicles and rail traffic from the mainland to the artificial island, is in the process of being built. Every year it will carry up to 25 million passengers to and from Kansai Airport.

Passengers will be conveyed on an automated guideway transit, a new device not found anywhere else in the world. It will be able to whisk 44,200 passengers a day to and from the aircraft gates located at each end of the terminal building.

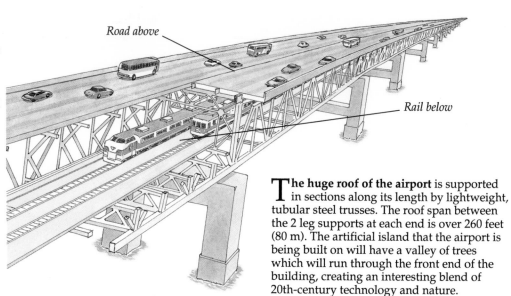

Road above

Rail below

The huge roof of the airport is supported in sections along its length by lightweight, tubular steel trusses. The roof span between the 2 leg supports at each end is over 260 feet (80 m). The artificial island that the airport is being built on will have a valley of trees which will run through the front end of the building, creating an interesting blend of 20th-century technology and nature.

To avoid the confusion of most airports, Kansai Airport will have passengers arriving at one end of the building and moving in a direct line to their aircraft.

Boarding bridge

KANSAI AIRPORT

KANSAI INTERNATIONAL AIRPORT in Japan, currently under construction, will be the world's first offshore airport. It was designed by Renzo Piano, who was one of the architects of the Pompidou Center. The terminal's smooth flowing lines imitate those of an aircraft. The airport is situated on an artificial 1,262-acre (511-ha) island 3 miles (5 km) off the east coast of Osaka Bay. Construction of the island began in January 1987, and the airport will be completed in the summer of 1994. The airport will have a runway of 11,500 feet (3,500 m), with a capacity for approximately 160,000 takeoffs and landings per year. When operational, an estimated thirty-one million passengers and 1.4 million tons of cargo will pass through Kansai Airport each year. The long-term plan is to increase the size of the airport-island to 2,964 acres (1,200 ha) and to add two more runways. The terminal building will be 945 feet (288 m) long, 492 feet (150 m) wide, and one of the largest buildings in Japan.

Site of airport

The island is settling by a process known as consolidation settlement, whereby water is squeezed out of the seabed subsoils by the weight of the landfill (earth and rubbish used to fill the site). In this way the subsoil forms a secure foundation for the airport. Building the airport offshore, away from built-up areas, solves the problem of noise pollution.

Roof trusses

Wing-shaped extensions

The interior of the passenger terminal building is open and spacious. The exposed trusses and the abundance of greenery inside emphasize the theme of technology and nature in harmony. The 3-story wings that extend to the north and south of the building incorporate the aircraft gates.

INTERNATIONAL AIRPORTS

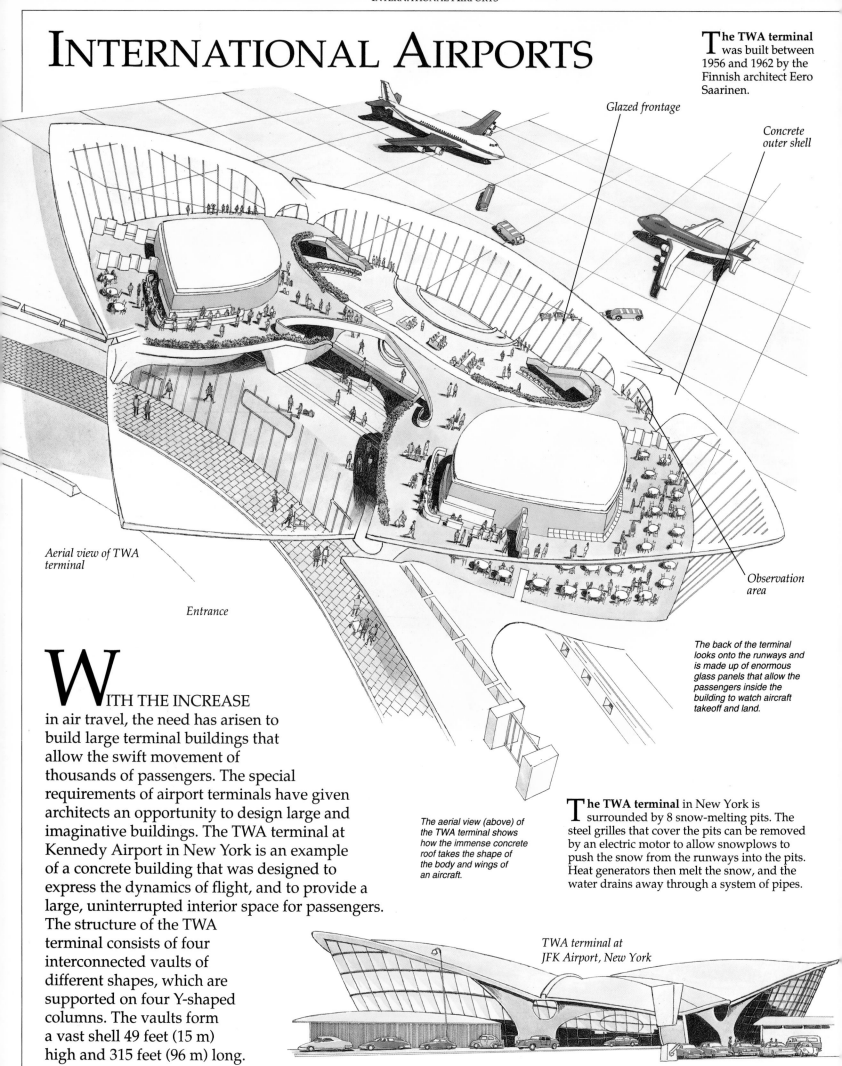

The **TWA terminal** was built between 1956 and 1962 by the Finnish architect Eero Saarinen.

Glazed frontage

Concrete outer shell

Aerial view of TWA terminal

Entrance

Observation area

The back of the terminal looks onto the runways and is made up of enormous glass panels that allow the passengers inside the building to watch aircraft takeoff and land.

WITH THE INCREASE in air travel, the need has arisen to build large terminal buildings that allow the swift movement of thousands of passengers. The special requirements of airport terminals have given architects an opportunity to design large and imaginative buildings. The TWA terminal at Kennedy Airport in New York is an example of a concrete building that was designed to express the dynamics of flight, and to provide a large, uninterrupted interior space for passengers. The structure of the TWA terminal consists of four interconnected vaults of different shapes, which are supported on four Y-shaped columns. The vaults form a vast shell 49 feet (15 m) high and 315 feet (96 m) long.

The aerial view (above) of the TWA terminal shows how the immense concrete roof takes the shape of the body and wings of an aircraft.

The **TWA terminal** in New York is surrounded by 8 snow-melting pits. The steel grilles that cover the pits can be removed by an electric motor to allow snowplows to push the snow from the runways into the pits. Heat generators then melt the snow, and the water drains away through a system of pipes.

TWA terminal at JFK Airport, New York

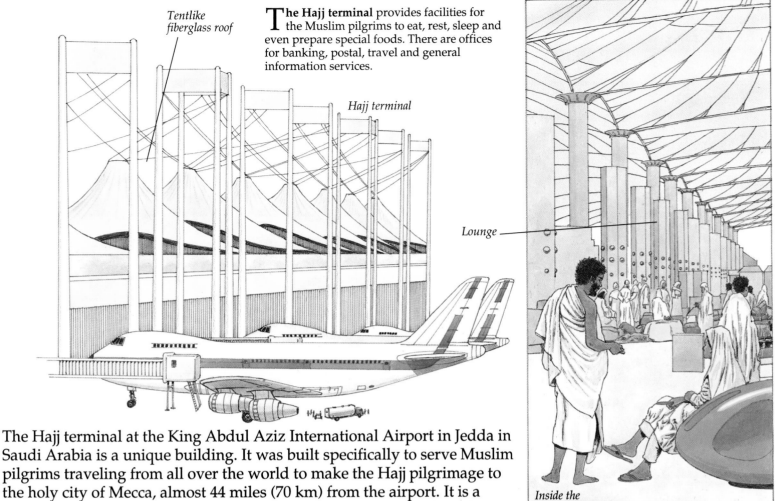

Tentlike fiberglass roof

Hajj terminal

The Hajj terminal provides facilities for the Muslim pilgrims to eat, rest, sleep and even prepare special foods. There are offices for banking, postal, travel and general information services.

Lounge

Inside the Hajj terminal

The Hajj terminal at the King Abdul Aziz International Airport in Jedda in Saudi Arabia is a unique building. It was built specifically to serve Muslim pilgrims traveling from all over the world to make the Hajj pilgrimage to the holy city of Mecca, almost 44 miles (70 km) from the airport. It is a journey that every Muslim is expected to make at least once in his lifetime. For a period of six weeks every year, the Hajj terminal provides shelter and facilities for an influx of almost a million passengers. As well as an air-conditioned building where the passengers are processed, and baggage collected, there is also a large, naturally ventilated building where passengers can rest and make their final preparations for the Hajj pilgrimage. Travelers are protected from the severe heat of the Middle East by a tentlike fiberglass roof covering. There are 210 "tent" roof units formed by steel cables at the top of 148-foot (45-m)-high columns. The result is a light, airy, uncluttered shelter that covers nearly 106 acres (43 ha).

The terminal at Stansted Airport in England also provides a large interior space for the flow of passengers. The long, low terminal of glass and steel attempts to recapture the atmosphere of a nineteenth-century railway station. Travel facilities and mechanical services are on the lower level, and the upper floor is left clear for the passengers.

Stanstead Airport was designed in 1986 by Norman Foster, who was also the architect of the Hongkong Bank. When planning Stanstead Airport, Foster took advice from many different areas. He involved the airport authorities, the head of a major airline, local government councils, and artists and designers. Foster carefully considered every aspect of the design of the airport, from the shape and height of the chairs in the lounges, to the enormous panes of glass which provide natural light, and the artificial lights which are cleverly hidden in the steel tree-like trusses that support the roof. The overall effect is of a giant "greenhouse" – an airport that is pleasing to look at and at the same time has an interior that is designed for efficient and speedy passenger transfers.

At Stanstead Airport the waiting aircraft are clearly visible from the passenger arrival and departure areas. The roof is made up of a series of shallow domes supported by tree-like tubular steel columns. The "trees" incorporate service pods that draw air, water and power from the floor below.

Stanstead Airport, England

TALLEST &Biggest

THE DESIRE TO BUILD huge, impressive structures seems to be common to all cultures throughout the ages. Structures such as the Egyptian pyramids, Greek temples, and the cathedrals of medieval Europe still inspire admiration. But the big buildings of the ancient world were structurally limited by the materials that were available at the time – wood, brick, and stone. A heavy stone structure could not be too tall or it would topple over. The tallest building of the ancient world was the Great Pyramid at Giza, which rose to a height of 482 feet (147 m). This may seem small in comparison with modern skyscrapers and towers, but the Great Pyramid held the record for the tallest structure for almost 4,000 years. It was overtaken by Lincoln Cathedral, England, in 1307, when, with the addition of a spire, the cathedral reached an overall height of 525 feet (160 m).

The illustrations on the following four pages compare the shapes and sizes of some of the largest buildings from around the world.

The **Twin Towers** (1) of the World Trade Center are situated on the southern tip of Manhattan Island. The towers are 110 stories high, and reach a total height of 1,348 feet (411 m). They are the tallest structures in New York City.

The **Louisiana Superdome** (2) in New Orleans was opened in 1975, and is the world's largest indoor stadium. It covers a total area of almost 10 acres (4 ha), and its dome covering is the largest ever built. The dome is 679 feet (207 m) in diameter and rises to a central height of 272 feet (83 m).

The **Paris Opera House** (3) in France was designed by Charles Garnier and was completed in 1874. It has a lavishly decorated façade of arched entrances, columns and statuary. A huge domed roof covers the central auditorium, and there is a maze of corridors running beneath the building.

Abu Simbel (4) in Egypt was built c. 250 B.C. to commemorate the reign of Pharaoh Rameses. The temple was carved 180 feet (56 m) into sandstone cliffs that run along the banks of the Nile. There were 4 statues of Rameses, each 66 feet (20 m) high, which guarded the entrance to the temple.

The **Eiffel Tower** (5) was built as the entrance archway to the Paris exhibition of 1889. This iron-and-steel tower was 1,000 feet (300 m) tall – almost twice as high as any structure that had ever been built. The Eiffel Tower was constructed in just two years, and it is one of Paris's most distinctive landmarks.

Cologne Cathedral (6) in Germany was begun in 1248, and although work continued on the cathedral for the next 2 centuries, the towers only reached the height of the nave. Building work started again in the 1860s, and the towers are now the second highest in the world – 515 feet (157 m).

The **stave churches** (7) of Scandinavia were constructed of wood, and their origin can be traced as far back as the Viking Age (A.D. 800–1100). This church, found in Borgund, Norway, is one of the best preserved and most authentic of stave churches. It has the characteristic stepped roof.

Himeji Castle (15) in Japan was built in the 16th century as a fortified residence during a period of civil war. The central building has several stories, each with curving eaves. The thick stone walls provided protection against artillery.

The Humber Bridge (14) in England was built between 1977 and 1981 and is the longest suspension bridge in the world – almost 9 miles (over 14 km). Two steel cables are carried over the top of the concrete towers and anchored on each side of the Humber estuary.

Iron Bridge (8), over the River Severn in England, was built between 1777 and 1779. It was the first successful cast-iron bridge, and was assembled from prefabricated parts which were joined together using dowels and dovetail joints. The Iron Bridge has a total span of 100 feet (30 m).

The Cathedral of St. Basil (9) in Moscow, Russia, was built between 1555 and 1560 by Ivan the Terrible. It was an expression of gratitude for the victory over the Mongolians, and is, in fact, nine separate churches; the main chapel being surrounded by eight smaller chapels.

The Colosseum (10) in Rome, Italy, was built from A.D. 70 to A.D. 81. It was the largest Roman amphitheater ever built – 164 feet (50 m) high, and 1,729 feet (527 m) in circumference – and held up to 50,000 spectators. Its massive structure was supported by arches and vaults, which also formed the seats.

The Basilica of Our Lady of Peace (11) in the Ivory Coast, Africa, was modeled on the design of St. Peter's Basilica in Rome. Our Lady of Peace is the biggest church in the world – 633 feet (193 m) long and 518 feet (158 m) high. It is made of marble, steel, concrete and glass and took just over two years to build.

The Pantheon (12) in Rome, Italy, was built by the emperor Hadrian between A.D. 120 and A.D. 124. The concrete walls are almost 20 feet (6 m) thick, and the dome is 141 feet (43 m) in diameter and height. The Pantheon has a 33-foot (10-m)-wide opening in the dome roof, which allows light into the temple.

Krak des Chevaliers (13) in Syria stood on a hill and was over 2,300 feet (700 m) high with walls that were nearly 82 feet (25 m) thick. The castle, which was the principal stronghold for the Crusaders, was occupied for the first time in 1109 and could hold up to 2,000 troops. The castle never fell to invaders.

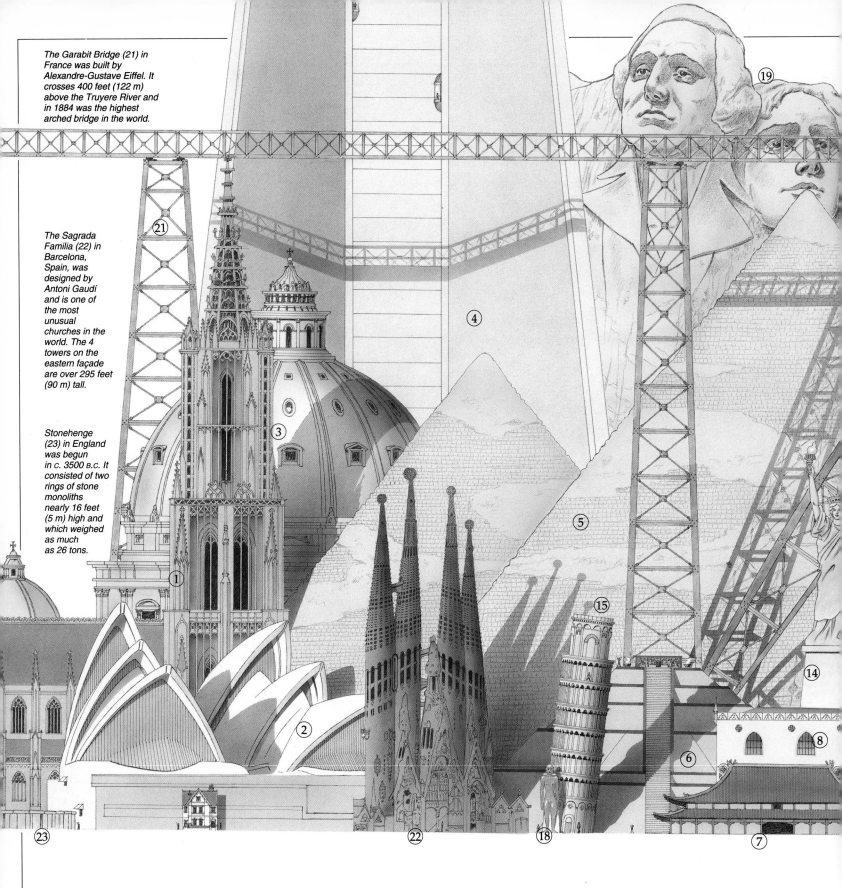

The Garabit Bridge (21) in France was built by Alexandre-Gustave Eiffel. It crosses 400 feet (122 m) above the Truyere River and in 1884 was the highest arched bridge in the world.

The Sagrada Familia (22) in Barcelona, Spain, was designed by Antoni Gaudí and is one of the most unusual churches in the world. The 4 towers on the eastern façade are over 295 feet (90 m) tall.

Stonehenge (23) in England was begun in c. 3500 B.C. It consisted of two rings of stone monoliths nearly 16 feet (5 m) high and which weighed as much as 26 tons.

Ulm Cathedral (1) is in southern Germany. It was begun in 1377 and building continued until the 16th century. The cathedral is 404 feet (123 m) long and 161 feet (49 m) wide. The spire was built between 1844 and 1890, and at 528 feet (161 m) high, it is the tallest spire in the world.

Sydney Opera House (2) in Australia is made up of a series of shell-like roofs. The building was constructed from prefabricated concrete ribs, which were bonded together with glue, and then strengthened with steel cables. The roofs are covered with millions of glossy and matte ceramic tiles.

The Basilica of St. Peter's (3) in Rome, Italy, was built between 1506 and 1626. This Roman Catholic cathedral is one of the finest examples of Italian Renaissance architecture. Its huge dome rises to a height of over 449 feet (137 m) and until 1989 St. Peter's was the largest church in the world.

The CN Tower (4) in Toronto, Canada, finished in 1975, is the tallest free-standing structure in the world. At 1,148 feet (350 m), there is a huge restaurant, with a revolving outer ring, and two observation platforms as well as broadcasting equipment. The antenna at the top reaches a height of 1,814 feet (553 m).

The pyramids at Giza (5), in Egypt, were built between the years 2660 B.C. and 2560 B.C. The largest pyramid is the one that was built as a tomb for pharaoh Cheops. The Great Pyramid, as it has come to be known, is still the largest stone structure in the world. It was originally 482 feet (147 m) high.

The Pyramid of the Moon (6) was built around A.D. 30 in what is now Mexico. The structure was almost 200 feet (60 m) high and 400 square feet (37 sq. m) at its base – which made it one of the largest pyramids in the Americas. The great pyramid was planned to be flat on the top in order to provide space for a temple.

TALLEST & BIGGEST

THE BUILDING MATERIALS and techniques of the modern world have freed architects from the constraints of traditional architectural forms. Thus we see the soaring lines of airport terminals that copy the shape of an airplane's wing, fantastic structures like the Sydney Opera House, and high-tech inside-out buildings, which are unique, and represent a complete break from any established architectural style. As construction technology advances, it is difficult to envisage the architectural wonders of the next century.

The surviving pagoda of the Yakusiji Temple (13), built around A.D. 680, is one of Japan's oldest buildings. This pagoda is 102 feet (31 m) high and has 3 main roofs and 3 lean-to roofs.

The Statue of Liberty (14) from its toes to the tip of its torch is over 151 feet (46 m) tall; it stands on a 151-foot (46 m)-high pedestal, bringing its total height to almost 305 feet (93 m).

The Leaning Tower of Pisa (15), Italy, was a bell tower. It was started in 1173 and completed in 1350. Because of ground subsidence the tower leans almost 13 feet (4 m) to one side.

The Geodesic Golfball (16) in Florida stands nearly 180 feet (55 m) high and has a diameter of 164 feet (50 m). Its dome is 16 feet (5 m) high and the structure rests on 3 pairs of legs.

The Motherland statue (17) in Russia holds the record as the world's largest full-figure statue. It is 269 feet (82 m) high and made of concrete.

The statue of Lord Bahubali (18) in India, was carved c. A.D. 981. It is 56 feet (17 m) high and is the tallest statue ever carved out of a single piece of rock.

Mount Rushmore (19) has the faces of 4 U.S. presidents carved into its side. Washington, Jefferson, Roosevelt and Lincoln. They are all 59 feet (18 m) high.

The Empire State Building (20) in Manhattan held the record for the world's tallest skyscraper for many years. It reached a total height of 1,472 feet (448.67 m). It took just over a year to build.

The Forbidden City (7) was the palace of Chinese emperors until 1922. This immense palace covered a total area of about 0.4 square mile (1 sq. km) and was made up of hundreds of single-story timber buildings. Entrance to this royal city was forbidden on pain of death to most ordinary people.

The Doge's Palace (8) is built on the canals of Venice, Italy. It was completed in the 14th century, and has 2 stories of arcades and delicate open stonework that support a marble façade. The total length of the Doge's Palace is 499 feet (152 m), and it is an example of Italian Gothic architecture.

Notre Dame Cathedral (9) in Paris, France, was begun in 1163 and was completed over 100 years later, in 1270. Notre Dame was one of the first Gothic cathedrals to be built. Its distinct twin towers rise to about 112 feet (34 m); its stained-glass windows are some of the largest ever built.

The Capitol (10) in Washington, D.C. was built between 1792 and 1830. It has an immense dome that rises as high as 230 feet (70 m). The Capitol combines classical Greek columns with modern American symbolism such as the Statue of Freedom that stands at the top of the dome.

The Temple of Amun (11) in Egypt was built from 1525 to 1212 B.C. In addition to the main temple, the walled enclosure of the temple contained a lake, 9 smaller temples and obelisks. The complex covers about 62 acres (25 ha), and it is the largest religious building that has ever been constructed.

The Parthenon (12) in Athens, Greece, was built by the ancient Greeks in the 5th Century B.C. and dedicated to the goddess Athena. It has a rectangular base, 240 feet (73 m) by 102 feet (31 m), and a colonnade on all four sides. The Parthenon was the largest and most beautiful of all the Greek temples.

THE X-RAY PICTURE BOOK OF BIG BUILDINGS OF THE MODERN WORLD # GLOSSARY

Apse The semicircular space at the east end of a church, usually behind the main altar.

Arch A curved structure used as support for a roof, bridge, etc., or as a decoration to a building.

Architect The designer of a building.

Atrium A large internal space within a building usually covered with glass.

Bascule A device that works like a seesaw. It is balanced so that when one end is lowered the other is raised.

Basilica A Christian church, rectangular in shape, with a long nave ending in an apse and flanked by colonnaded aisles.

Beam A piece of a building's structure, that usually runs side-to-side

Brace A strengthening piece of wood or iron used as a support in a building

Caisson A permanent substructure that is sunk below the ground or into the seabed to protect workers against the collapse of soil or sudden water leakage as they excavate. After bedrock is reached, the caissons are filled with concrete to become foundations.

Canopy A rooflike covering that is suspended over a bed, throne or other object.

Cast iron A mixture of iron and carbon produced by smelting ores. It is poured, or cast, into molds. Cast iron is hard and brittle and cannot be shaped by hammering or rolling because it will break.

Centenary The hundredth anniversary.

Chinoiserie The Chinese style of furniture and decoration.

Clay A kind of soil, powdery when dry; workable and sticky when wet.

Column A pillar; a slender upright structure used as a supporting or an ornamental feature in a building.

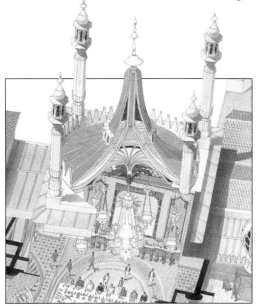

Concrete Cement mixed with pebbles, crushed stone, sand, and water.

Dolly bar A tool used to hold a rivet at one end while a head is hammered out of the other end.

Dome A rounded vault forming a roof.

Foundations The base of a structure, often below ground level, carrying the weight of the building.

Gasolier An early ornamental chandelier with branches ending in gas jets.

Granite A very hard rock which is gray to pink in color.

Great Depression The economic slump that began in 1929 and continued until the late 1930s. During this period there was widespread unemployment.

Hajj The pilgrimage to the Holy City of Mecca that every Muslim is expected to make at least once in his lifetime.

Hydraulic Operated by the movement of water through pipes or channels.

Industrial Revolution The change in society, occurring first in Britain in the eighteenth century, caused by the development of machinery and large-scale factory production. As a result of the Industrial Revolution, the vast majority of the working population moved from agriculture to industry.

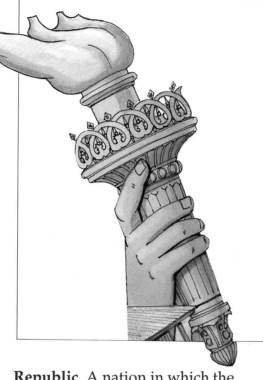

Iron A metallic element of great strength found throughout the earth's crust in the form of ore. When the iron is purified and mixed with other materials it is known as steel.

Medieval Characteristic of the Middle Ages, which was the period from about 1100 to 1500.

Minaret Inspired by Islamic architecture, these are usually tall, slender towers often attached to a mosque, from which Muslims are called to prayer.

Mogul Coming from the 15th- and 16th-century Mogul Empire in India.

Mosaic A painting usually made up of small pieces of colored stone.

Nave The main part of a church, between the side aisles.

Obelisk A tall, four-sided stone pillar that tapers towards its pyramid-shaped top.

Pavilion An ornamental building used for entertainment.

Plantain A tropical tree related to the banana tree and bearing similar fruit.

Portland cement A type of cement which is made from chalk and clay and can set hard under water.

Pylon A tall structure erected for support.

Republic A nation in which the supreme power rests with all the people or their elected representatives and not with a monarch.

Rib A projecting band in a vault used for structural or decorative purposes.

Rivet A nail or bolt for holding metal components together. Its head end is beaten out or pressed down when in place.

Scaffolding A structure put up temporarily around a building during construction work.

Shell structure A double or single curved syrface used as a structural support.

Steel A metal made by reducing the carbon content of iron. Other ingredients may be added to give steel different characteristics, such as hardness and toughness.

Strut An iron or wooden bar placed in the framework of a building to carry weight or pressure.

Stucco Plaster or cement used for coating walls.

Terra-cotta Unglazed, baked clay used for construction and decoration, as well as in statuary and pottery.

Tracery Stone ornamental work with a decorative pattern of interlacing or branching lines.

Truss A framework of bars or beams that supports a roof or a bridge.

Turret A small tower connected to, yet projecting from, a building, usually at a corner, and often only ornamental.

Vault An arched ceiling, roof, or covering of masonry.

Wrought iron A type of iron made by heating cast iron in a refining furnace to draw off some of its impurities. It is easy to work and can be formed into many shapes. Wrought iron does not have great compression strength, so it tends to buckle under heavy loads.

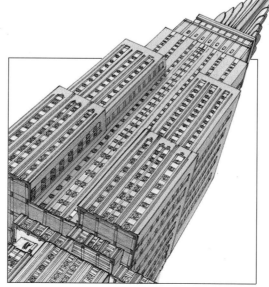

ACKNOWLEDGMENTS

The Salariya Book Co. Ltd wish to thank the following people for their assistance:

Stella Bedoe — Keeper of Decorative Arts Royal Pavilion, Brighton, England.

Chigusa Oshima — Chief of International Affairs Division – Kansai Airport, Japan.